MIND-BLOWING FUN FACTS ABOUT MARRIAGE AND DIVORCE

"I Now Pronounce You Fun & F*cked",
Marriage & Divorce Facts
Not taught at the Altar-
With Interpretations and Moral Lessons.

NICCI BROCHARD
&
BEN CHUBA

MIND-BLOWING FUN FACTS ABOUT MARRIAGE AND DIVORCE

"I Now Pronounce You Fun & F*cked",
Marriage & Divorce Facts
Not taught at the Altar-
With Interpretations and Moral Lessons.

Book Formatting by: *Monish*

Book cover design by: *Danish*

CROSSBORDER

New York, London, Quebec

CONTENTS

Introduction 1

Chapter 1: Honeymoon Hangover: When "Happily Ever After" Gets Real 3

Chapter 2: The Great Divide Chores, Bills, And the Fine Print of Married Life 34

Chapter 3: Spice And Slump: The Truth About Sex and Intimacy After 'I Do' 41

Chapter 4: Meet The In-Laws (And Outlaws): Family, Friends, And the Social Circus 46

Chapter 5: For Better or For Children – Parenting, Not Parenting, And Marriage 52

Chapter 6: From "I Do" To "What The?!" – Bizarre Marriage Customs & Historical Facts 59

Chapter 7: Happily, Never After? – Surprising Facts on Divorce and Aftermath 67

Chapter 8: Till Debt Do Us Part the Real Cost of Marriage (And Divorce) 75

Chapter 9: Where To Go – Travel, Living, And Escaping the In-Laws 89

Chapter 10: How To Move on: Divorce, Dating Again, And Fun Facts from The Other Side 97

Introduction

So, you've picked up a book with a title that probably made you snort-laugh in public. Good. That means you're precisely the kind of person who needs what's inside these pages: brutal honesty wrapped in humor, statistics that will make your jaw drop, and wisdom no one bothered to share before you signed that marriage certificate or divorce papers.

Welcome to **"I Now Pronounce You Fun & F*cked"** – where we cut through the tulle, champagne toasts, and Pinterest-perfect expectations to expose the raw, unflinching reality of matrimony and its sometimes inevitable conclusion.

Let's be clear: this isn't your grandmother's advice book. Those cutesy "keys to a happy marriage" guides belong on the same shelf as fairy tales. Instead, think of this as the unauthorized user manual; the one that explains why your relationship "check engine" light keeps flashing despite following all the conventional wisdom.

Did you know that couples who spend over $20,000 on their wedding are 1.6 times more likely to divorce than those who spend under $10,000? Or that the average divorced person waits just 3.7 years before taking another swing at marriage? How about the fact that the profession with the highest divorce rate isn't "rock star" or "professional athlete" but rather gaming managers and bartenders?

These aren't just quirky factoids to share at dinner parties. Each statistic reveals profound truths about how we approach commitment, what we value, and where we routinely go wrong. This fun fact book covers hundreds of such revelations, each accompanied by interpretations that might make you uncomfortable and moral lessons you probably won't find on inspirational wall art.

This is straight to you who are single, engaged, married, divorced, or some complicated relationship status that Facebook hasn't invented a category for yet, this fun filled book is beyond entertainment. It's armor. Knowledge. Power.

So buckle up. Things are about to get educational... and just a little bit f*cked.

Honeymoon Hangover: When "Happily Ever After" Gets Real

In an idyllic 1848 painting, newlyweds glide across a Norwegian fjord in a bridal boat procession, epitomizing the romantic ideal of sailing off into "happily ever after." But once they dock back in real life, even those couples had more to unpack than just luggage. Fast forward to today: the wedding confetti has settled, the Instagram #BigDay posts are live, and you're finally home from the honeymoon. You might expect wedded bliss to kick in on day one yet instead, you feel a tad... hungover. If so, you're not alone. In one study, over 50% of new brides reported feeling sad or let down after the wedding. This emotional dip often dubbed the "post-wedding blues" or honeymoon hangover is a real phenomenon that catches many couples off guard.

Why does this happen? Simply put, the fairy tale collides with reality. All the anticipation, planning, and excitement surrounding the wedding create a high that's hard to sustain. After the "I do," you're suddenly faced with everyday life routines, bills, quirks, and maybe an ominous pile of dirty laundry on the floor. The contrast can be jarring and even humorous. One minute, you're dancing in a tux and gown; the next, you're arguing about the proper way to squeeze the toothpaste tube. Early marriage is a time of adjustment, where expectations meet reality in often eye-opening ways.

This chapter tackles the honeymoon hangover head-on by exploring seven hard truths (with a wink and a smile) about the realities of early marriage and post-wedding life. Don't worry it's not all doom and gloom. Each section blends a bit of history or culture (who knew the original "honeymoon" wasn't so sweet?), relatable anecdotes of newlywed misadventures, and a few stats and studies to show that you're far from alone. More importantly, we'll draw out the moral lessons for newlyweds like adjusting expectations and practicing patience and empathy and offer practical solutions for each challenge (from carving out alone time to keeping love handles in check). We'll do it all with an engaging, humorous tone because laughing together is one of the best ways to survive the early bumps of marriage.

By the end, you'll hopefully see that imperfection is normal, those "am I doing this right?" moments are universal, and that love can evolve into something deeper and more beautiful than the fairy tale even if it doesn't always resemble a Disney movie. So, let's dive into the seven realities that can give any couple a honeymoon hangover and how to handle them with grace and good humor.

1.The Original "Honeymoon" Wasn't So Sweet

We tend to think of the honeymoon as a blissful vacation with your spouse mojitos on the beach, rose petals on the hotel bed, and nonstop romance. Culturally, it's painted as one of the sweetest times in a marriage. But here's a reality check that might surprise you: the term *honeymoon* originally had a much more cautionary meaning. In fact, the very word was coined to suggest that the first month of marriage is sweet like honey but quickly wanes like the phases of the moon. Yes, you read that right. Built into the word is the idea that the initial glow of love inevitably fades as time passes. Not exactly the "endless bliss" promised in travel brochures.

A bit of history here; the concept of the honeymoon has evolved significantly. The modern custom of jetting off after the wedding only became common in the 19th century. Before that, "honeymoon" referred to a period, not a destination. Early references from the 1500s and 1600s describe it as a fleeting interval of love and happiness. In other words, even our ancestors knew that once the wedding feast and merry making ended, everyday marriage with all its quirks would begin. Perhaps medieval newlyweds also discovered that their beloved's snoring could rival a dragon's roar once the castle lights went out.

And if you think your in-laws are challenging, consider this historical tidbit: some sources say the honeymoon began as a literal hideout. In certain cultures, there was a practice of "marriage by capture," where a groom would abduct his bride and hide with her for a lunar month so her family couldn't retrieve her. During this month, they'd presumably drink mead (honey wine), possibly to encourage conception and solidify the union. By the time they re-emerged, the bride would be pregnant and the marriage unavoidable. Not exactly two weeks in Maui, right? It's a darkly comic contrast: today's couples fret over all-inclusive resort packages, while ancient grooms worried about angry fathers with swords. The original honeymoon wasn't sweet or glamorous it was practical, sometimes tense, and understood to be temporary.

So how does this help modern couples? It's a reminder to temper our expectations. If even the word for "marital bliss vacation" carries an implicit warning that the sweetness won't last forever, we can cut ourselves some slack for feeling let down when the real world intrudes. After the high of the wedding and a dreamy honeymoon, it's normal to experience a comedown. You get home and life is waiting: the fridge is empty, the thank-you cards need writing, work is calling, and your spouse's adorable habit of singing in the shower is less charming at 6 A.M. on a weekday. The transition can be bumpy. Psychologists note that many newlyweds experience uncertainty and blues in this phase. It's a classic case of expectation versus reality.

The Moral: Happily ever after isn't an automatic setting it's a journey. The end of the wedding is the beginning of a marriage, and like any journey, it comes with highs and lows. Knowing that even in folklore the honeymoon was seen as fleeting can actually be reassuring: if you come home and feel a bit of a "honeymoon hangover," you're not failing at marriage you're just human. Love isn't a constant vacation;

it's a real-life adventure with chores, responsibilities, and learning curves. The key is to embrace the transition instead of mourning the end of the all-honey-no-moon phase.

Practical solutions for the honeymoon hangover

- **Plan small joys after the big day:** Don't let the wedding and honeymoon be the only peak moments of excitement. Schedule a fun outing or mini getaway a few months into marriage or take up a new hobby together. Having something to look forward to can ease the post-wedding blues and keep your bond fresh.

- **Set realistic expectations:** Daily life will resume laundry, grocery runs, work emails and all. Talk openly about how you'll divide responsibilities as a team before resentment has a chance to brew. Better yet, turn mundane tasks into shared time cooking dinner together with music on can be surprisingly romantic.

- **Keep the romance alive in little ways:** The Caribbean may be behind you, but "honeymoon moments" can still happen at home. Schedule a regular date night, light candles at dinner on a random Tuesday, or declare a no-phones, movies-in-bed Sunday. Intentional connection often outlasts fairy-tale spontaneity.

- **Talk about the blues:** If one or both of you feel a slump post-wedding, don't bottle it up. Share openly without blame. You might find your spouse is feeling just as off-kilter. Talking it out can bring perspective and even spark a laugh at how anticlimactic real life feels after such a high. If the sadness lingers, consider speaking with a counselor. Remember, emotional hangovers often signal that something meaningful just happened (your wedding!), not that something is wrong.

By recognizing the honeymoon as a beautiful, temporary bubble, you can refocus on building something deeper and more lasting. You weren't meant to stay on the moon forever there's a whole earth of shared experiences waiting once you land.

2.The Seven-Year Itch (and Sooner)

You've probably heard of the "seven-year itch", that fabled point in marriage when spouses supposedly grow restless, bored, or eager for change (sometimes, unfortunately, in the form of affairs or divorce). The term gained fame thanks to the 1955 Billy Wilder film *The Seven Year Itch* best known for Marilyn Monroe's skirt flying up over a subway grate in which a married man's eye begins to wander after seven years of monogamy. But is the seven-year itch real? And do we really have to wait that long for the honeymoon glow to fade?

Reality check: many couples feel the relationship heat cool much earlier sometimes as soon as seven months or even seven weeks (like when you realize in month one that your spouse considers pizza an acceptable breakfast every day). The "itch" is often less about a specific year and more about the natural evolution of a relationship once the novelty wears off.

That said, statistics do show a notable trend around the 7–8-year mark. In the U.S., the average duration of marriages that end in divorce is about eight years, lending credence to the "seven-year itch" as a real phenomenon. One *Psychology Today* analysis noted Census Bureau data showing that first marriages ending in divorce last around 8.2 years on average. So, there is something to that timetable, many couples hit a wall of dissatisfaction or restlessness in the mid-single digits of marriage. Why? Relationship experts point to several factors. By this time, couples may have young children (hello, sleep deprivation and endless diaper changes), full-blown careers, and mounting financial responsibilities, a far cry from the footloose dating days. Romance can get buried under the weight of daily logistics. Personal development can also create friction; many people undergo significant growth or changes in their late 20s to early 30s, making the partner you married at 25 feel quite different by 32.

In fact, some psychologists suggest adults tend to grow and change in roughly seven-year cycles, which can rock the boat in long-term relationships. As therapist Robert Taibbi explains, around the fifth to eighth year of marriage, one or both partners may experience a period of restlessness; questioning life goals, craving new experiences simply because human needs evolve over time. It's less "I don't love my spouse" and more "I feel stuck in a routine" or "Who am I now versus who I was?" If couples don't recognize this as a normal developmental phase, they might mistakenly attribute it entirely to the marriage hence the "Did I marry the wrong person?" worries that can arise (more on that in the next section).

But here's an even earlier reality: you don't have to wait seven years to feel an itch. Plenty of couples report the initial passion easing after a year or two. The giddy butterflies of new love settle into steadier affection. It's not that you don't love each other; it's that our brains simply can't sustain the intense infatuation stage indefinitely. Studies on marital satisfaction have found that for many couples, happiness declines over the first few years of marriage as the "honeymoon phase" ends. One long-term study of newlyweds showed that while the number of marital problems didn't necessarily increase, couples' satisfaction still tended to drop in the first four years. In other words, you might still have the same lovable (and annoying) partner you did on day one ; they're not doing more wrong, but your rose-colored glasses have come off, and those issues that seemed tiny early on now feel larger. The perception shifts. This normal adjustment can happen well before year seven, which is why some joke about the "two-year itch" or how marriage can shift from fireworks to sparklers to a comfy glow within the first few anniversaries.

The Moral: Don't fear the seven-year itch as some marriage doom prophecy. Understand that relationships naturally wax and wane in passion and satisfaction over time. Itchiness, whether it's a desire for novelty, space, or change is often a sign your marriage needs a tune-up, not a trade-in. It's like hitting cruise control on a road trip: even a scenic drive can make your eyes droop after a while. You might need to switch drivers, change the playlist, or pull over and stretch not abandon the car on the highway. In marriage terms, that means proactively injecting novelty and addressing simmering issues before they boil over.

How to navigate the itch (at 7 years or any time)

- **Regularly "check in" on your marriage:** Don't wait for a crisis to evaluate how each of you is feeling. Every few months, have a candid chat: What's going well? Any pet peeves brewing? Is there something either of you longs to do (individually or together) that you haven't? These talks can catch an itch early, before it becomes a rash.

- **Keep dating each other:** It's classic advice because it works. Especially as routines set in, make an effort to plan date nights or new experiences. Try a new restaurant, take a weekend trip, or even just switch up your Friday movie genre. Novelty releases dopamine; the same "falling in love" brain chemical. Research shows shared **exciting activities boost marital satisfaction** by rekindling that early-stage excitement.

- **Pursue individual growth (and share it):** Seven-year itch feelings often stem from personal stagnation. Encourage each other to pursue hobbies, friendships, or learning opportunities. If you're feeling alive and growing as individuals, you bring that energy back into the marriage. Take an art class, join a sports league, or start a small side business – and cheer each other on. You'll have fresh things to talk about and mutual pride.

- **Refresh your environment:** Sometimes the itch is as simple as being tired of the same four walls or routines. Redecorate a room together, rearrange the furniture, or even consider a change of scenery if feasible (move apartments or take an extended travel sabbatical). A literally fresh coat of paint in your life can symbolize a new chapter together, staving off boredom.

- **Remember commitment and why you married:** During an itchy period, nostalgia can actually help. Reminisce about your early days – flip through the wedding album or watch your ceremony video, laugh at how young or sappy you looked. Reminding yourselves of your love story's start can strengthen your resolve to write its middle and end together. Some couples even renew vows around year 7 or 10, which can be a beautiful way to reaffirm your commitment and celebrate how far you've come (despite any itches along the way).

Importantly, if the itch manifests as serious thoughts of infidelity or divorce, consider seeking marriage counseling sooner rather than later. A professional can help both partners uncover underlying needs or frustrations and find constructive ways to address them. Many marriages emerge from the seven-year itch stronger than before, like a phoenix rising from the flames once couples confront their issues and rediscover their bond. The truth is marital satisfaction often rebounds after the challenging early years; one large study found that couples tend to become happier from around the 10-year mark onward. So hang in there and work through those itchy moments together, the best may be yet to come.

3. Alone Time? What Alone Time?

One of the biggest adjustments after moving in together as a married couple is the sudden disappearance of "alone time." Remember when you could spend a Saturday playing video games or reading a book for five hours straight without anyone wondering if you'd died? Or when "me time" meant a quiet evening journaling or soaking in the tub? In early marriage, those solitary pleasures can become rare creatures indeed. Newlyweds often joke that privacy becomes a luxury; whether it's having your spouse constantly in your space or well-meaning friends and family inviting you both to every event now that you're a packaged deal. The reality of sharing your life so closely is that you're almost never alone. And that togetherness, while lovely can sometimes feel a tad overwhelming.

In many cases, it's a blessing that you always have a partner by your side, literally. Movie night? You've got a built-in buddy. Woke up at 3 a.m. from a nightmare? There's someone there to groggily reassure you. Even trips to the grocery store become duo activities. But the flip side is that alone time both personal alone time and quality "just us two, no others" time now requires more intentional effort. Ironically, "alone time" can mean two different things for newlyweds: the time each individual needs by themselves (say, one spouse goes for a run while the other watches a favorite show), and the time the couple needs alone together, away from external demands. Both tend to shrink after the wedding.

Why does personal alone time diminish? For starters, you're likely living together (perhaps for the first time). That means waking up together, going to bed together, eating most dinners together basically, another human is in your domestic space 24/7. It's wonderful for intimacy, but if you're someone who recharges alone, you might start feeling mildly claustrophobic. Picture an introvert who married an extrovert: the introvert might crave an hour of silence after work, while the extrovert is eager to chat about their day. Or vice versa one spouse gets lonely easily and always wants to do things jointly, leaving the other thinking, "Can I just have ten minutes to scroll mindlessly in peace?" Even if you love each other's company, constant togetherness is an adjustment. One husband quipped that after marriage he couldn't even sit on the toilet in peace without his wife knocking to ask where the extra toothpaste was. "Alone time? What alone time?" he joked. "Even my shadow has company now."

The couple-alone-time issue arises when you realize marriage often pulls you into a swirl of social and family obligations. Maybe while dating, you guarded your weekends for romance. Now, Aunt Marge expects you at Sunday dinner, your parents want more visits ("bring that lovely spouse of yours!"), and friends assume you'll join every group outing as a pair. It can feel like you have less one-on-one time than before you tied the knot. Some newlyweds even find themselves missing their own spouse that is, missing quality time with them because work, chores, and social events eat up all the hours. You're always around each other, but not necessarily connecting meaningfully. Alone-together time can slip through your fingers if you don't protect it.

The Moral: Marriage is a balancing act between togetherness and individuality. Finding that balance is crucial. Being joined at the hip might sound romantic, but in practice, a bit of breathing room is healthy. You're still two individuals with unique needs, even as you grow into a single unit. As the saying goes, "I can't miss you if you're never gone." Small doses of absence really can make the heart fonder or at least prevent you from wanting to strangle each other over trivial annoyances. Likewise, carving out couple-alone time (just the two of you, no others) is essential to keep romance and intimacy strong, especially as your social circles merge and grow. The key is communication and boundaries: openly discussing your needs for personal space or more one-on-one time without taking it as rejection or offense.

Strategies for reclaiming alone time (for you *and* for two):

- **Communicate your need for "me time"**: This can be delicate, and you don't want to hurt your spouse's feelings, but a loving partner will understand that needing alone time doesn't mean you love them less. Frame it positively: "I recharge by having a little quiet time, so I'm going to go read for half an hour – it helps me be more present with you afterward." Or establish a routine: "Every Saturday morning, I'd like to go for a solo bike ride; maybe you can have your time to sleep in or do your thing, and then we'll meet for brunch." When both people voice what they need, you can negotiate a win-win.

- **Designate personal spaces or times in the home**: If space allows, each spouse might have a corner or room that's *their* zone (e.g., a desk, a workshop table, a reading nook). Even in a small apartment, maybe one gets the living room for an hour while the other hangs in the bedroom, then swap. Some couples implement an unofficial "do not disturb" signal by wearing headphones or closing a door to indicate "I'm in my bubble for a bit." Respect those signals. It's not a snub; it's self-care.

- **Plan couple-only dates and trips:** To get that treasured *alone-together* time, sometimes you have to put it on the calendar. Have a rule that, say, Thursday nights are just for the two of you, no friends, no family, no distractions. You might cook dinner together and then talk or watch a movie, but the point is bonding without outside interference. Similarly, consider the occasional "staycation" weekend where you two turn down other invitations and focus on each other. It might feel weird to schedule time with your own spouse, but busy lives demand intentionality. Protecting that time pays off in closeness.

- **Set boundaries with loved ones:** Families and friends are important, but they need to learn that you're a unit with your own schedule now. It's okay to say, "We're not available this weekend – we have plans," even if the plan is to chill at home together. Early on, establish polite boundaries: maybe alternate holidays between families, or limit how many social events you commit to each week, so you don't overextend. The people who care about you will understand that sometimes the couple needs solitude. (And if they don't, well, consider it practice in united-front boundary setting as a married team!)

- **Embrace parallel play:** Sometimes you want to be near your spouse *but* still technically doing your own thing – that can count as quasi-alone time. Perhaps one of you is painting or gaming on one side of the room while the other is reading or doing yoga on the other. You're together, but not in each other's hair. This can be very comforting – the companionship is there, without constant interaction. You can even head to a coffee shop together and sit at separate tables working on individual projects. Get creative in finding ways to co-exist with a bit of personal breathing room.

Finally, remember that needing time apart is normal. In fact, psychologists say that a healthy dose of personal space can strengthen a relationship by preserving each partner's sense of self and reducing petty frustrations. When you reunite, even after just an afternoon apart, you often feel refreshed and genuinely excited to see each other.

As for missing the absolute privacy of single life: yes, it's an adjustment to share everything (you'll learn more about your partner's bathroom habits than you ever wanted to know). But over time, many couples find a comfortable rhythm where togetherness and alone time flow naturally. You begin to read each other's moods and offer space or closeness as needed. And sometimes, you'll discover that choosing to spend your free time with your spouse even when you could be alone becomes your preference. That's a sign your marriage has evolved into a true partnership, where being alone is nice, but being with your best friend in comfortable silence is even nicer.

4. "Did I Make a Huge Mistake?" Moments

Picture this: It's 2 a.m., you and your spouse just had a ridiculous fight over whether the comforter should be tucked or untucked, and now you're lying awake thinking, *"Oh no… Did I make a huge mistake?"* If you've had a moment like this, welcome to the club population: pretty much every married person at some point. Those *"what have I done?!"* flashes of doubt can ambush even the most in-love newlyweds. Maybe it's triggered by a fight, or by noticing an irritating trait in your partner you swear wasn't there before (they snort when laughing?! How did I miss that in three years of dating?!). Or perhaps nothing in particular happened you just wake up one day with a sinking sense of finality, like *"This is it, forever? Gulp."* It's a scary thought.

First, let's normalize it: experiencing moments of doubt is common in the early stages of marriage. The transition is huge you've legally, emotionally, and financially tied your life to someone else's. It's not unusual to have occasional panic moments, kind of like buyer's remorse after a big purchase only amplified because, well, this "purchase" can talk back and leave socks on the coffee table. In fact, researchers Laura Stafford and Allison Scott found that new brides who experienced "post-wedding blues" often questioned the relationship, with some wondering if they'd made the right decision in marrying their partner. These doubts can creep in surprisingly early. One anonymous wife described how "doubts first began to creep in during our honeymoon" as minor annoyances ballooned: *I thought he was arrogant; he thought I was clingy.* Yikes imagine thinking you married the wrong person before the thank-you notes are even mailed!

What causes these "huge mistake" moments? A few things. Conflict is a major one. The first big blow-up as a married couple can feel earth-shattering. You might think, *We never fought like this before did we rush into this?* In reality, you're likely just facing issues that were easy to dodge during dating but are unavoidable in marriage like how to spend money, deal with in-laws, or allocate free time. Conflict can make you temporarily question compatibility. Stress is another culprit moving in together, combining finances, and adjusting to each other's habits can create pressure that sparks second-guessing. And then there's the sheer permanence of marriage. Psychology calls it "commitment panic." It's not that you want out but the realization that you *can't* easily get out can trigger a natural what-if reflex. Think of it like standing at the base of Mount Everest: you wanted to climb, you're excited to climb but looking up at the massive mountain, it's only natural to think, *Can I really do this? Was this a mistake?*

Culturally, the phrase *I think I made a huge mistake* has become a punchline (thanks to TV shows like *Arrested Development*, where G.O.B. blurts it out comically). But in real life, it can feel dark and shameful to admit. Rest assured, having fleeting doubts doesn't mean your marriage is doomed or that you actually married the wrong person. A UK survey by a life insurance company found that about one in three married Britons have some regrets about their marriage or choice of spouse. That doesn't mean one in three will divorce it means that over the years, people naturally reflect on paths not taken or imperfections in their partner. Humans second-guess big decisions whether it's buying a house or choosing a career and marriage is no different.

The Moral: Don't confuse a bad moment or a tough phase with a bad marriage. In other words, don't panic. The presence of doubts simply means you're evaluating your situation honestly. What matters is how you respond to those thoughts. Rather than berating yourself (*"How could I think such a thing? I'm awful!"*) or jumping to drastic conclusions (*"We had a fight, we shouldn't be married!"*), treat the doubt as a signal to look closer. Ask: *Why am I feeling this way? Is there a solvable problem here, or am I just overwhelmed and scared?* Often, it's the latter. And like any fear, talking about it with your spouse or a trusted friend can shrink it back down to size.

How to handle the "huge mistake" moments

- **Zoom out before you freak out:** In the heat of doubt, try to mentally step back and view the situation in context. Did you marry a good person whom you love and respect, and are you just having a rough week? Chances are yes. Remind yourself of the positive history you share and the reasons you committed. One disagreement or annoying discovery (e.g. he chews really loudly) doesn't erase the love. It helps to recall, *this is just a moment*, not the whole story.

- **Talk it out carefully:** If the doubt stems from a specific issue (say, "We keep fighting about money, did I make a mistake marrying someone with different spending habits?"), it's actually productive to voice that concern to your spouse in a constructive way. For example, "When we argue about finances, I get scared because I worry we're fundamentally incompatible. I know that's dramatic, but it's how I feel. Can we find a better way to get on the same page with money so I can put that fear to rest?" This kind of vulnerable sharing can be hard, but a supportive partner will want to reassure you and work on the issue. If the doubt is more of a vague feeling, you might talk to a wise friend or a counselor first rather than blurting it to your spouse and hurting them. Hearing someone say, "Yeah, I wondered that too at one point, it passed," can be hugely reassuring.

- **Avoid comparison traps:** Doubts often worsen when we compare our marriage to others'. Be wary of idealizing another couple or the notion that "others don't struggle like this." Social media is not real life, the smiling honeymoon pics and anniversary tributes don't show the behind-the-scenes conflicts. Every couple has *something* to work through. Also, don't compare your spouse to an ex or an imaginary "perfect partner." You married this person for a reason. No one on Earth could fulfill 100% of your fantasies (sorry!). Recognize that some disappointment is actually about realizing *no* partner is perfect, not that *your* partner is uniquely flawed.

- **Give it time:** Early marriage is a huge adjustment. If you hit a rough patch at month 6 and think "mistake!", commit to revisit the feeling in a few months. You might find with more time, things improve, and the doubt was just jitters. Obviously, this excludes serious issues like abuse or severe infidelity – those need immediate action. But for normal doubts, patience is key. Think of it like a new job – the first few months you might question if you're cut out for it; by month 12 you feel much more competent. Similarly, once you and your spouse survive some challenges together, you'll likely feel more secure that, yes, this marriage can withstand turbulence.

- **Work on yourself:** Sometimes doubts about your partner are projections of internal stuff. Are you unhappy with *yourself* in some way? Did you expect marriage to magically fix your insecurities or provide nonstop happiness (see section 6 ahead)? If so, the "mistake" was not marrying them, but thinking they'd save you from you. Recognize if you have personal issues; anxiety, trust issues, unrealistic expectations that need addressing. Do the self-work (with therapy if needed). As you grow more content personally, minor flaws in your partner often become far easier to accept, and doubts fade.

In summary, those "Did I blow it?" thoughts are usually like passing dark clouds. Don't make permanent decisions (or accusations) under their shadow. Many longtime married couples will tell you they had early moments of doubt that now make them laugh. What matters is that unless you're facing true deal-breakers, commitment means choosing to stay and work through it even when your feelings wobble. On the other side of a resolved conflict or a period of growth, you often find your love strengthened and your confidence renewed: *"No, I didn't make a mistake. We've got this."*

And if the doubts persist or deepen, that's okay too it may signal deeper issues that can be addressed with professional support. One of the great truths about marriage is that it's less about finding a "perfect" match and more about building a resilient partnership. Imperfections and second thoughts are part of the construction process

Love Handles and Letting Go

You've probably heard the term "love handles" those extra inches that settle around the waist. Well, don't be surprised if a few of those handles arrive as uninvited wedding gifts! Early marriage often coincides with a bit of "letting go" in the personal upkeep department. During courtship and wedding prep, many people are in top form hitting the gym, watching their diet, always dressing to impress on date nights. After marriage, however, there's often a subconscious relaxation of effort. You've won each other's hearts, so why agonize over six-pack abs or full makeup every day? Suddenly, Friday nights shift from dining at that trendy bistro in a slim-fit outfit to wearing matching sweatpants, ordering pizza on the couch, and binge-watching Netflix with zero shame. Comfort replaces formality both in behavior and, often, in physical shape. In short, many couples get a bit chubbier and sloppier together and honestly, that can be one of the sweet joys of intimacy: not feeling the pressure to be "on" all the time. But it does come with health and self-esteem considerations to keep in mind.

Let's talk stats for a moment (in case you think we're exaggerating this weight gain trend). Multiple studies have documented the "newlywed spread." One study found that young spouses who were very satisfied in their marriage gained more weight in the early years than less-satisfied ones. That's right being happily married can literally fatten you up! Researchers humorously theorized that content couples feel less motivated to maintain a svelte figure because they're not out there looking for a mate they've already got one. Meanwhile, less happy spouses (perhaps subconsciously keeping an eye on the exit door) tended to keep their weight in check, maybe to maintain "market appeal." It's a funny reversal of the usual assumption that a good relationship is always healthy for you. In this case, it seems "I love you just the way you are" can morph into a mutual agreement that an extra taco or two won't hurt until repeated indulgences start to challenge your jeans' button.

Check this out: In early 2025, research found that marriage triples the risk of obesity in men and significantly increases the odds of being overweight for both genders. Specifically, married men were 3.2 times more likely to be obese than their single counterparts, and their risk of being merely overweight was 62% higher. Women didn't show a spike in obesity, but their odds of being overweight rose by 39% compared to unmarried women. That tracks with common experience: the husband relaxes a lot (hello, beer belly and dad bod), while wives often try to uphold certain standards but may still gain a bit. And if pregnancy enters the picture, more pounds may follow and bouncing back can be tough for mom (while dad often sympathy-eats along the way).

But it's not just weight. "Letting go" in marriage can also mean relaxing some of the polite pretenses you kept during dating. Maybe you used to never burp in front of your partner now you two belch the alphabet and laugh hysterically. Or you stopped dressing to the nines; your spouse mostly sees you in old band T-shirts and that ratty robe. Personal grooming might slide a bit skipping shaving, forgetting cologne. The flame of passion might not burn as spontaneously; maybe you both scroll on your phones in bed instead of snuggling. You've gotten comfortable. The urgency to impress has faded, replaced by a cozy assurance that "we love each other, so take me as I am morning breath and all."

There's good and bad in this. On one hand, how wonderful to be so secure that you can be your authentic, comfy self-that's intimacy. On the other hand, if taken too far, it can lead to complacency, which might dim attraction or energy over time. Health-wise, carrying extra weight into later years can pose risks (heart disease, diabetes, etc.), so the cumulative effect of all those pizza nights needs consideration. And emotionally, while no one should feel pressure to look like a magazine cover for their spouse, a little effort in maintaining appearance and romance can go a long way in keeping mutual attraction alive. It's about finding balance between "I love that I can wear PJs around you" and "I still want to wow you on occasion."

The Moral: Love isn't about looks but health and effort still matter. The lesson for newlyweds is that while it's perfectly normal (and delightful) to ease up on strict diets and always being in seduction mode, you shouldn't completely "let yourself go" to the point of neglect. Marriage isn't a finish line after which you stop trying. Think of it as a journey where you want to be healthy and confident for each other and where a bit of effort shows care. This applies both physically and emotionally. Yes, you can rock those love handles proudly (your spouse might even find them cute!), but make sure you're also taking care of your body for the long haul. And keep tending the garden of romance even if you're gardening in sweatpants.

Keeping love (and yourselves) in shape:

- **Stay active together:** Instead of seeing exercise as a solo chore, turn it into quality couple time. Take evening walks hand-in-hand, go biking on weekends, sign up for a dance class or doubles tennis. Not only does this help combat weight gain, but it can also be fun and bond-strengthening. Studies indicate couples who exercise or engage in physical activities together tend to be more satisfied with their relationship and find it easier to maintain healthy habits (accountability buddies!). Even a shared morning stretch or yoga session in the living room can start your day with both fitness and closeness.

- **Mindful eating (with room for treats):** Cooking at home is often healthier than constant takeout – and it can be a romantic activity. Try making meals together and learning new recipes. You can light candles and make a date out of a random Tuesday dinner. Aim for balance: incorporate veggies and nutritious foods so that those pizza-and-ice-cream nights remain special treats, not the nightly default. If you do notice the scale creeping up in a way that bothers you or affects your health, have an honest, non-judgmental talk about re-calibrating your diet together. Team up to pack lunches or gently remind each other of goals (e.g., "Let's skip dessert on weekdays, and save it for Saturday date night").

- **Small efforts in appearance:** Again, no one is suggesting you need a red carpet look at home. But little things like changing out of the ratty pajamas occasionally, or wearing that nice cologne/perfume on your at-home date, can reignite sparks. It tells your partner, "You're worth making an effort for." Maybe surprise your spouse by dressing up a bit for an at-home dinner, or keep up with grooming habits that you know make you feel confident and attractive. It's as much for you as for them when you feel good about how you look, you bring positive energy. And yes, complement each other! If your wife puts on a cute outfit for date night, *tell her she looks beautiful.* If your husband got a fresh haircut or is wearing that shirt you love, *let him know he's looking handsome.* Positive reinforcement 101.

- **Embrace the comfy, but keep some mystery:** Part of letting go is losing all mystery and while transparency is generally good, a bit of mystique can keep romance alive. It's okay to close the bathroom door and not overshare every bodily function. Maintaining some boundaries like this preserves a *romantic* image of each other beyond just roommates who know every unglamorous detail. Surprise each other now and then – it can be as simple as the spouse who usually lounges in sweats putting on jeans and doing their hair on a Saturday, or planning a surprise date. These things prevent the relationship from feeling too stale or predictable.

- **Encourage each other kindly:** If you notice your partner is feeling self-conscious about weight gain or has slipped into a funk of not caring for themselves, approach it with empathy. A supportive comment like, "Hey, I've been thinking of getting back to working out, would you like to do a fitness challenge together?" works better than, "You've put on weight, maybe you should hit the gym." Likewise, celebrate healthy choices they make: "I love that we're cooking more veggies, I feel so good!" When you treat it as a joint venture for mutual benefit, it doesn't turn into nagging or hurt feelings. You both want each other to *thrive.*

Ultimately, the goal is to enjoy the comfort of marriage without sliding into unhealthy complacency. It's about striking a balance wearing those matching flannel PJs on Sunday morning, and still dazzling each other now and then on a Friday night. And remember aging and body changes are natural. Love handles may come and go, hairlines may recede, and metabolisms may slow. Part of the beauty of marriage is loving each other through all those changes.

A common joke among long-married couples is, *"We got fat and old together, and it's been great!"* The key word is *together*. Supporting each other in staying well and laughing off the superficial stuff ensures that a few extra pounds here or there don't weigh down the relationship itself.

Marriage Won't Fix You

It's a tale as old as time (or at least as old as Hollywood rom-coms): a lonely or flawed person meets their soulmate, marries them, and *poof!* all their personal problems disappear in the warm glow of happily-ever-after. If only real life worked like that! One of the hard truths newlyweds often learn is that marriage doesn't magically fix your personal issues or erase pre-existing relationship problems. If you were insecure, anxious, prone to jealousy, struggling with debt, or had a habit of leaving wet towels on the floor saying "I do" doesn't cast a fix-it spell. In fact, those issues often become *more* visible when you're sharing a life 24/7. As relationship experts often quip, "Whatever baggage you had before, you bring it into marriage and now it's unpacked in the middle of your living room."

Many of us consciously or not harbor a hope that marriage will "complete" us (shout-out to Jerry Maguire's famous line, "You complete me"). We think finding that one true love will fill emotional voids, heal traumas, motivate personal change, or resolve long-standing conflicts. "Once we're married, he'll stop partying so much," or "She'll be less anxious once we settle down." That's a heavy set of expectations to place on matrimony, and reality tends to disappoint. Research actually shows that entering marriage believing it will solve your problems is risky. One study found that many newlyweds held overly optimistic expectations assuming marriage would boost self-esteem, happiness, and stability only to later discover those beliefs didn't match reality. The core issues individuals or couples faced before often persist after the honeymoon ends.

Consider a couple who fought frequently while dating. They think getting married will cement their bond and end the insecurity but after the honeymoon, they're still bickering, maybe even more, as they now have more logistics, decisions, and stress to juggle. Or take someone with unresolved trauma or mental health challenges who believes love will heal them. While a supportive spouse can provide comfort, they are not a therapist or a cure. Sometimes, the excitement of new love temporarily masks depression or anxiety but once the novelty fades, those conditions often resurface. In fact, research suggests that after the initial post-wedding happiness spike, people tend to return to their pre-marriage emotional baseline. If you were a "glass-half-empty" person before, odds are you'll still see some half-empty glasses after even if your partner is wonderful.

Another common misconception is that marriage will "fix" the relationship itself. Maybe there were trust issues or red flags during dating, but one or both partners believed tying the knot would resolve them that commitment would automatically spark better communication or mature behavior. Unfortunately, a wedding band isn't a magic ring (and if it were, let's not forget that Frodo's ring didn't bring out the best in people). If underlying issues weren't addressed before, they'll follow you into marriage often with higher stakes.

The Moral: Marriage is not a cure-all. It's a partnership, not a personal rehab program or a conflict eraser. The key is to avoid the "I'll be fixed when…" trap. Happiness, personal growth, and healthy relationship dynamics require continuous self-work and, sometimes, outside help not just a wedding vow. Your spouse can walk beside you on your journey, but they can't carry you up the mountain of your own struggles. In fact, expecting them to can put unnecessary strain on the marriage. The healthiest couples are made of two people who take responsibility for their own well-being while supporting each other, not expecting the other to fix them.

How to grow *with* your spouse, not expect them to fix you:

- **Work on issues *before* marriage (and after):** If you're reading this as a newlywed, you're already past the "before" part, but it's worth noting for context. Ideally, couples should address major issues (addictions, chronic conflicts, value differences) in premarital counseling or serious talks. But if you didn't, don't despair, just acknowledge that these require work now. Identify personal areas you each want to improve. Maybe one of you has anger issues, the other has trouble with honesty ;lay it on the table and consider seeing a counselor or setting up strategies together. Rather than finger-pointing ("You need to change this about yourself"), make it a team effort ("How can I help you cope with your anxiety better? And here's how you can help me stick to a budget," etc.).

- **Don't outsource your happiness:** It's easy to lean on your spouse as your sole source of joy or confidence, but it's healthier to maintain a sense of self. Continue hobbies, friendships, and interests that fulfill you individually (remember the alone time discussion!). This takes pressure off the marriage to be *everything*. If you struggle with something like low self-esteem, certainly your spouse's love is a huge boost, but you might also benefit from personal practices; journaling, therapy, achievements at work or creative projects that build your self-worth from the inside. Think of your partner as your cheerleader, not your savior.

- **Shared growth mindset:** It helps tremendously when both partners agree, "We're each a work in progress, and marriage is a journey of growth." That way, when flaws or issues surface, you see them as challenges to tackle together, not reasons to blame each other. If one of you had a bad habit (say, shutting down during arguments), discuss it openly and set mutual goals to improve communication. Maybe even read marriage self-help books or take a workshop together – approaching improvement as a united front can be even kind of fun, like a project. Crucially, practice patience. Change doesn't happen overnight just because you both said, "I do." Celebrate small improvements and be forgiving of relapses.

- **Use "we" language but own your part:** When dealing with a problem, avoid the trap of *"you* need to fix this." Instead, try *"we* can work on this," while still acknowledging individual responsibility. For example, instead of "You're depressed, you need help," one might say, "I've noticed we haven't been as happy lately; maybe we can both make our mental health a priority; I'll support you if you want to talk to someone. I might talk to someone too to learn how to help better." This aligns you as partners tackling an issue, not opponents. Studies show that approaching marriage as a *team* (using "we" and seeing problems as shared) correlates with better outcomes and marital stability.

- **Seek professional help when needed:** There is zero shame in getting help; whether it's individual therapy for personal issues or couples therapy for relationship issues. In fact, doing so early can prevent small cracks from becoming canyons. A therapist can give you tools to manage anxiety, trauma, or conflict that love alone might not solve. Think of it as adding tools to your marriage toolbox. If your spouse is struggling with something you can't fix (e.g., deep-seated self-esteem issues or a lingering grief), encourage them lovingly to seek counseling, offering support like handling insurance or scheduling if they feel overwhelmed. Going together to couples counseling can also be great; it's like a tune-up for the marriage engine. Far from being a sign of failure, it shows a commitment to make the marriage as strong as it can be.

To drive the point home, consider this bit of anecdotal wisdom from countless long-married couples: *"Marriage doesn't make your problems go away it sometimes amplifies them."* For example, if someone has a temper, sharing close quarters offers more opportunities for that temper to flare. If someone struggles with insecurity, marriage might initially soothe it (*"Finally, someone chose me forever!"*), but over time, every missed call or busy day can reignite those feelings.

The good news? Marriage can also provide a safe space, at least in a healthy relationship, to face those issues with a loving partner by your side. The happiest couples aren't the ones with zero problems; they're the ones where each person commits to becoming the best version of themselves, and helps their partner do the same, through all the inevitable messiness.

So instead of expecting marriage to fix you, think of it as a supportive environment where you can grow with encouragement, accountability, and unconditional love from your number one fan.

Reality vs. Expectations

Every love story begins with expectations. We walk into marriage carrying visions of what it will be like often shaped by movies, social media, our parents' relationships, or pure fantasy. We might expect endless cuddles, a partner who intuitively understands us, a picture-perfect home, a passionate sex life uninterrupted by exhaustion, and a happily-ever-after version of our dating life minus the uncertainty. Then reality arrives, bags in hand, ready to move in. And we discover sometimes hilariously, sometimes painfully the gap between reality and our expectations. This is the overarching theme of the honeymoon hangover: realizing that "happily ever after" doesn't mean *perfectly* ever after.

Consider a few common expectation-versus-reality moments: You may have expected to gaze lovingly at each other over candlelit dinners each night in reality, you're scarfing down cereal in front of the TV, too tired to talk. You expected sex every other day now that you live together reality reminds you that stress, mismatched libidos, and sleepiness exist. You expected adoration and patience at all times reality is they have moody days and may snap over something minor. You expected to take on everything as a team reality hits with job loss, illness, or a pandemic (hello, 2020), and tests your teamwork in unexpected ways. Even external expectations buying a house, having Pinterest-worthy kids can unravel under financial constraints or fertility challenges. The gap between dream and day-to-day can feel like a letdown.

Unmet expectations are one of the leading causes of marital conflict and dissatisfaction. Much of the early frustration in marriage doesn't stem from egregious behavior but from your partner not meeting an expectation you never clearly expressed. For example, maybe you expected them to help with chores without being asked because, to you, that's what a "good spouse" does but they figured you enjoyed doing them since you always took the lead. Or perhaps you thought marriage would mean never feeling lonely again, only to realize your partner can't be there 24/7 and you wrongly blame the marriage for not fulfilling you completely.

Unrealistic or unspoken expectations set you up for disappointment. In fact, holding idealized visions of marriage has been identified as a major risk factor for marital distress. When you expect perfection or a fairytale script, you create a standard that no real marriage no matter how loving can meet.

So, what's the remedy? Adjust, communicate, and appreciate. Adjust your expectations to be realistic and flexible. Communicate them clearly don't assume your partner "should just know." And appreciate what *is* instead of fixating on what *isn't*.

Take this quick anecdote: A newlywed wife assumed her husband would continue the grand romantic gestures of their engagement surprise flowers, elegant date nights. Months into marriage, she's disappointed by their absence. In her mind, "A good husband should always woo his wife." Meanwhile, he thought things were great they cuddle and say "I love you" daily, so he assumed the grand gestures were mostly for the proposal phase. Once they talked it out, he realized she was craving a little more intentional romance. He began sprinkling in surprise notes and picnics. She adjusted her view from "weekly wow moments" to "meaningful daily affection with occasional romantic extras." Both felt more fulfilled.

The Moral: Expectations need reality checks. That doesn't mean abandoning all standards kindness, respect, and emotional safety are always fair to expect. But knowing the difference between a fair expectation and a fantasy is crucial. Embrace the marriage you *have* messy, flawed, and deeply real not the one you imagined or saw online. Reality may be less polished, but it holds its own unexpected beauty. Maybe you didn't expect cleaning the garage together to become a bonding moment filled with laughter, but it is. Maybe you didn't expect that loving someone deeply would also mean getting really mad at them then working through it and coming out stronger. But that, too, is love the resilient kind.

Bridging reality and expectations:

- **Be explicit about expectations:** Many expectations lurk unspoken until they're violated. Avoid that by discussing them early. Sit down and literally share, "What does being a husband/wife mean to you? What roles do you expect us each to play? How do you envision holidays, or conflict resolution, or social life as a married couple?" You might be surprised where you differ. It's much easier to negotiate expectations in advance ("Oh, you assumed we'd visit your parents every Sunday; I assumed we'd alternate, let's figure out a plan") than to be silently disappointed later. This is an ongoing process, too – expectations about careers, children, etc., should be revisited as life evolves.

- **Embrace a realistic narrative:** Rewrite your internal story of marriage to be more realistic. Instead of "We'll never fight if we're truly in love," tell yourself "Even loving couples fight; what matters is we fight fair and make up." Instead of "We must always make each other happy," think "We strive to make each other happy, but we're also responsible for our own happiness." Adjusting the narrative removes the pressure that you *should* be living a perfect Instagram-worthy life. A dose of humor helps – e.g., expect that there will be days where the most romantic thing your spouse says is "I took out the trash." That's okay!

- **Focus on what's working:** When reality doesn't match expectation, it's easy to zoom in on the negative (the things you *aren't* getting). Make a conscious effort to notice and appreciate the good that is there. Maybe your partner isn't as tidy as you hoped, but they are an amazing listener when you're stressed. Or your house isn't as big as you wanted by now, but it's full of warmth and laughter. Practicing gratitude – even literally writing down a few things you're grateful for in your spouse each week – can shift your perspective to see that reality, while not perfect, is pretty great in many ways. Many couples say that what they *actually* got (an imperfect but genuine companionship) is ultimately more satisfying than what they *thought* they wanted (a flawless fairy tale).

- **Adjust together when possible:** If an expectation is truly important to one of you, see if you can meet in the middle. Maybe you expected a lavish joint vacation every year, but finances make that hard – perhaps you plan a cheaper getaway or fun staycation instead, to keep the spirit of that expectation alive. Or if one expected a very active sex life and the other's drive is lower, you communicate and find a frequency and timing that works for both, maybe incorporating more non-sexual intimacy too. Being open about these things prevents resentment. It's not about *lowering* expectations to zero, but *adapting* them to fit your unique dynamic and finding creative alternatives.

- **Kill the comparison beast:** Nothing skews expectations like comparing your marriage to others. If you see friends seemingly living a dream (traveling a lot, or spouse always buying gifts, etc.), remember you're seeing a curated slice. Every marriage has trade-offs. Social media is especially guilty of triggering "expectation inflation"; suddenly you expect to do elaborate anniversary surprises because you saw someone else do it. By all means, get inspiration, but don't let it dictate what your marriage *should* be. Focus on what *you two* value. Maybe you realize you don't actually care about fancy anniversary dinners (that was an external expectation); you'd rather go hiking or play board games to celebrate, because that's more "you." That's perfectly fine! There's no one-size-fits-all marriage.

In essence, the dance between reality and expectations is one you'll keep doing throughout your marriage. The goal isn't to erase all expectations, but to keep them flexible and rooted in open communication. Over time, many couples find that their expectations naturally become more realistic and better aligned with their unique relationship and that shift often leads to greater satisfaction. In fact, research shows that marital happiness tends to increase later in life as couples settle into adjusted expectations and more defined roles. They accept each other's imperfections and find a rhythm that works.

The sooner you can make that mental shift from idealization to appreciation the more peace and joy you'll cultivate in your marriage. Because while reality may not look like a fairy tale, it *is* the story you two get to write together and that's far more meaningful than any pre-written script.

Conclusion

As we reach the end of this chapter, take a deep breath of relief: you've survived the myth-busting tour of early marriage realities! By now, it's clear that the honeymoon hangover that sobering adjustment from fantasy to reality is something virtually all couples experience in one form or another. If some (or all) of the seven facts resonated with you, rest assured: these challenges are normal. They're not signs your marriage is broken or "wrong." Imperfection is the name of the game when it comes to human relationships and thank goodness for that, because who could live up to perfect?

Think of marriage not as the finale of a fairy tale, but as the beginning of a more complex, yet deeply rewarding, story. It's less *"happily ever after"* and more *"happily enough, day by day, with effort and love."* The beauty lies in how love evolves beyond the sparkly surface. Those early butterflies might settle, but in their place can grow a solid foundation of trust, humor, and intimacy richer and deeper in many ways. The annoying quirks become inside jokes. The hardships you endure together become badges of honor that strengthen your bond. The question isn't whether your marriage will face difficulties it will but whether you'll face them as a team and learn from them. Each time you communicate through a misunderstanding, support each other through an "itch," or forgive a mistake, you prove your love is real and resilient.

Let's recap a few key takeaways: Love alone doesn't guarantee a smooth marriage it takes communication (about everything from chores to fears), patience (with your partner's growth and your own), and consistent effort (to keep romance alive, carve out time, and show appreciation). It also takes empathy recognizing that your partner is going through the same adjustment you are, and offering each other grace. When you find yourself thinking, *"Marriage shouldn't be this hard,"* remember anything worthwhile takes work. As the saying goes, a smooth sea never made a skilled sailor and by navigating these early marriage storms, you're becoming seasoned captains of your relationship.

Statistics and studies can offer useful insights like how satisfaction dips then rises, or how common certain hurdles are but every marriage is unique. You and your spouse get to define your own version of "happily ever after." Maybe it's not glamorous. Maybe it includes squabbles, stretch marks, and Saturday nights folding laundry but if it's built on understanding, laughter, support, and deep affection, which sounds pretty happy to me.

With each challenge overcome from carving out alone time to weathering doubts you're earning small victories that, over time, add up to a profound confidence: *We can handle whatever life throws at us.* That's a powerful foundation.

So, to all the newlyweds (and not-so-newlyweds) reading this: embrace your imperfect, real love story. Let go of the pressure to live a highlight reel, and invest instead in the messy, beautiful process of growing together. When *"ever after"* gets real, don't run lean in. Laugh at the absurd moments (they make the best stories), learn from the hard ones, and love each other through them all.

Because at the end of the day, the post-honeymoon phase while devoid of fairy dust holds something even better: a genuine, evolving connection grounded in reality. And that kind of love the kind that sees and accepts the real you, and still says *"I choose you every day"* is far more magical than any fairy tale.

Cheers to evolving love and many decades of growing old playfully love handles and all together. You've got this. And more importantly, you've got each other. That's more than enough for a truly happy ever after.

CHAPTER 2

The Great Divide: Chores, Bills, And the Fine Print of Married Life

Marriage is a beautiful, complex beast. It's built on love, yes, but also on to-do lists, monthly bills, and passive-aggressively reloaded dishwashers. It's less *riding off into the sunset* and more *trying not to murder each other over how to fold fitted sheets*. This chapter is your backstage pass to the gritty (and often hilarious) reality of domestic married life.

Spoiler: it's not all roses and surprise getaways. It's more like split grocery bills, co-owned Wi-Fi plans, and the eternal question *who left the cap off the toothpaste… again?*

Here, we dive into seven fun (and surprisingly revealing) facts about how couples navigate the seemingly mundane but secretly monumental realms of chores, finances, and everyday habits. Think of this as marriage's "fine print": the clauses nobody reads before signing, but everyone ends up living by.

Chores Rank High on the Marriage Priority List

Let's just rip the Band-Aid off: doing chores is sexy. Or at least it's sexy-adjacent. According to surveys, sharing household chores ranks just below fidelity and good sex on the list of what makes a successful marriage. Yes, you read that right; doing the dishes is basically in a throuple with trust and bedroom chemistry.

While movies love to highlight romantic candlelight dinners, they rarely show who's scraping wax off the tablecloth afterward. In real married life, desire can be slowly strangled by a mountain of dirty laundry. A sink full of moldy Tupperware? Absolute mood killer. And nothing makes you question your life choices quite like realizing your partner thinks "wiping the counter" means pushing crumbs behind the toaster.

Couples who get this right treat chores like a team sport. It's not about personal preferences (because let's face it no one loves scrubbing toilets). It's about fairness, consistency, and mutual respect. When your partner grabs the vacuum without being asked, it doesn't just clean the floor it clears out resentment too.

Mini Anecdote: Emma and Jake, married six years, finally found peace after Jake started doing the dishes nightly. "It's weird," Emma says, "I used to feel invisible. Now, when I see him in the kitchen after dinner, I suddenly want to make out with him by the spice rack." Forget roses get yourself a partner who scrubs the pan

Fairness = Happiness

Fairness in marriage is like Wi-Fi when it's working, you don't notice it. When it's not, everyone's miserable.

Studies show that when wives perceive household labor as fairly divided, they report higher levels of marital satisfaction. And no, this doesn't require 50/50 spreadsheet-level precision it's about *perceived* fairness. The effort and intention behind the task often matter more than the task itself.

There's something deeply romantic about a partner who steps up without being asked. You know what's *not* romantic? Having to remind someone eighteen times that the recycling goes out on Thursday. Even if you whisper it while wearing lingerie it's just not hot.

What's more, husbands who share household responsibilities actually spend more quality time with their spouses. The logic? When the workload is balanced, there's more time (and emotional bandwidth)

to enjoy each other's company without simmering resentment bubbling under every "How was your day?" conversation.

Funny Truth Bomb: Cleaning the shower drain voluntarily? That's the new love language. It's the "acts of service" upgrade nobody knew they needed.

And fairness isn't just about chores it's emotional, too. If one person is always the one planning vacations, scheduling the kids' dental appointments, and coordinating family holidays, that invisible labor adds up fast. The result? One partner feels drained and underappreciated, while the other is left wondering why there's "tension" all the time.

So yes, fairness isn't about keeping score it's about saying, *"Hey, I see what you're doing, and I've got your back."*

Everybody Fights About Chores

If you've ever argued about how to fold a towel, congratulations: you are *very* married.

Nearly 80% of couples fight about housework. The top three fights?

1. **Who** should do it

2. **When** it should be done

3. **How** it should be done

That last point deserves its own TED Talk. Because let's be honest: everyone has a *way*. There's a correct direction for toilet paper (over, obviously). There's a proper dishwasher strategy (knives down, glasses on the top rack). And don't even get started on what qualifies as "clean" when it comes to bathroom mirrors.

But these disagreements aren't really about cleaning they're about control, communication, and compatibility. That fight over whether to vacuum before or after guests arrive? It's actually a skirmish about expectations, habits, and the household scripts we absorbed growing up. Welcome to the psychological minefield of adult cohabitation!

Mini Anecdote: Sam and Priya spent an entire Saturday silently feuding over how to organize their spice rack. The issue? Alphabetical vs. usage frequency. They ended up with two racks. Peace was restored though the cinnamon now lives in exile.

Here's the thing: these fights are *normal*. And oddly comforting. They mean you're building something real. You're not just playing house you're actively negotiating what "home" means to each of you. The key is to laugh when you can, compromise when you must, and always remember: a mismatched sock is not a declaration of war.

For Richer, For Poorer: Money Trouble Ahead

Let's talk about the third rail of relationships: money.

It's not sexy. It's not poetic. But it's very, *very* real. In fact, money issues are the third leading cause of divorce right behind infidelity and incompatibility. And honestly, sometimes money causes both.

Early in marriage, financial conversations often go like this:

"We'll just figure it out!"

Translation: *"We have no plan and are hoping love magically pays the electric bill."*

Whether you're both savers, spenders, or a mix of the two, transparent communication about money is essential. And yet many couples avoid the topic until it explodes usually in the form of a surprise $300 drone purchase, or a hidden credit card statement tucked behind the coffee filters.

Funny Truth Bomb: That cute little *"what's mine is yours"* vow? It didn't mention overdraft fees or accidentally signing up for four streaming services.

Here's a helpful mindset shift: think of your finances like a shared garden. You both need to water it, weed it, and occasionally prune back your partner's obsession with limited-edition sneakers.

Mini Anecdote: Tasha and Neil saved their marriage by committing to monthly "money dates." Just one hour, two glasses of wine, and one spreadsheet. It wasn't romantic, but it was bonding, and it saved them $600 a year in duplicate subscriptions. Boom

Work vs. Wife (or Husband)

Marriage doesn't stay at home it follows you to work. And not just emotionally. Companies lose an estimated $6 billion annually in productivity due to employees' marital issues.

Ever tried focusing on a Zoom call while mentally replaying a 7 a.m. spat about who forgot to pack the kids' lunches? Exactly. A rocky marriage leaks into everything emails, deadlines, office banter. It's like carrying a thundercloud in your briefcase.

But here's the flip side: happy marriages = productive employees. Studies show that when home life is stable, workers bring more focus, energy, and collaboration to their jobs. Basically, love at home can mean promotions at work.

Mini Anecdote: Marcus, an ad exec, swears his recent raise was indirectly thanks to a marriage therapist. "Once we figured out how to stop fighting about groceries, I started sleeping better. My pitch meetings got sharper. Boom bonus!"

So, if you're managing a team and one employee seems "off"? Maybe they're not lazy maybe they're emotionally steamrolled by last night's argument over whether or not to get a dog.

Marriage Can Make (or Break) Your Bank

Marriage is weirdly financial. On average, married couples accumulate **four times** more wealth than their single counterparts. Why? Shared resources, joint decision-making, and a sense of long-term planning.

But here's the twist: divorce can wipe out those gains. Divorced individuals have **77% fewer assets** than singles. That's a shocking number but it reflects legal fees, asset splits, and the emotional and financial toll of starting over.

In essence, marriage is like a startup. When it works, you grow together and build capital both emotional and literal. When it fails, the crash can be brutal (and expensive).

Funny Truth Bomb: Breaking up may be hard to do, but breaking up your 401(k)? That's where the real tears begin.

This doesn't mean you should stay in a miserable marriage for the money. But it does mean that working through the hard stuff when it's safe and respectful can bring more than just emotional rewards.

The Chore Gap Lives On

Even in 2025, the "chore gap" is still alive and kicking. Despite modern ideals and shared income, studies show women still do significantly more housework and childcare even when working full-time jobs.

That doesn't mean husbands aren't trying. It just means cultural habits die hard. Many men think they're doing 50%, but when time-tracked, they're actually hovering around 30%. Oops.

Women often serve as the de facto household managers keeping track of birthdays, groceries, dentist appointments, clean socks, and family group chats. That invisible labor adds up, even if it's not on the chore chart.

Mini Anecdote: Lena once asked her husband to "help with the kids' school stuff." He showed up to one PTA meeting, got a cookie, and declared, "I'm crushing this dad thing!" Lena just stared.

The fix? Awareness, honesty, and course correction. You can't close a gap you don't admit exists.

Final Thoughts: In Messiness and in Health

Marriage isn't one big decision; it's a thousand tiny ones, made together (or occasionally, passive-aggressively via Post-it notes). It's a delicate dance of love, logistics, and learning that sometimes, yes, taking out the trash is a love story.

So next time you're fighting over dish placement or credit card bills, take a breath. You're not doing it wrong you're just doing the real work of being married.

And who knows? Maybe the secret to a lasting relationship isn't in romantic poems or beach vacations, but in shared spreadsheets and knowing the *correct* way to fold a towel.

Spice And Slump: The Truth About Sex and Intimacy After 'I Do'

Let's face it few topics are as giggle-worthy, eye-roll-inducing, or myth-laden as sex in marriage. You hear it all: the steamy tales of newlywed bliss, the cautionary jokes about marital dry spells, the sitcom tropes of "headaches" and separate beds. But what's the truth once the honeymoon haze fades and "real life" rolls in?

This chapter pulls back the covers on married sex and intimacy, diving into seven cheeky yet revealing facts that expose the quirks, pitfalls, and surprising perks of post-"I do" bedroom life. Prepare for laughs, nods of recognition, and maybe a few raised eyebrows.

So much for "Saving It" Until Marriage

Once upon a time, the wedding night was the big reveal the moment the veil dropped, literally and figuratively. But in today's world, the surprise factor is, well, mostly gone. A whopping 85% of couples have already had premarital sex by the time they say their vows. That makes the wedding night less about discovering each other's bodies and more about staying awake mid-snog after a chaotic day of celebrations and forced family photos.

Forget rose petals and lingerie reveals. Most modern couples enter marriage already well-versed in each other's preferences, quirks, and go-to positions. Which, in many ways, is a win. There's less pressure and more comfort. Still, the myth of the magical wedding night lingers in movies and media. In reality, it often involves a late-night fast-food run, peeling off uncomfortable outfits, and vowing to "do it properly" after some sleep.

When the Honeymoon Suite Goes Cold

Two years in, the candles might still be on the nightstand but now they're covered in dust. Around one in five couples is already having sex fewer than ten times per year just two years into marriage. That's not just a dip it's practically sex hibernation.

Roughly one-third of American marriages fall into the "low-sex" or "no-sex" category. It's a stat that shocks many but makes sense once you factor in the avalanche of life post-wedding: careers, bills, chores, kids, aging parents, and those Netflix marathons that somehow win out. Add the emotional labor of partnership and caregiving, and sex can start to feel like another item on the to-do list not exactly a turn-on.

But here's the twist: a lull in sex doesn't mean a lack of love. For many, intimacy morphs into shared laughter, quiet comfort, and stolen cuddles. Still, don't underestimate the toll a long-term dry spell can take. As we'll explore, physical closeness matters far beyond the moment.

The Real Average Sex Life

Let's bust a big myth: married couples are not doing it every night. In fact, the average is 58 times a year just a little more than once a week. So if you and your spouse aren't swinging from ceiling fans every evening, congrats you're totally average.

This stat can be weirdly comforting. Many couples secretly worry they're "not normal" if they're not constantly in the mood. But between 9-to-5 jobs, PTA meetings, grocery runs, meal prep, and general life grind, maintaining weekly intimacy is actually impressive.

The truth is that quality trumps quantity. A satisfying, emotionally connected experience once a week can do more for a marriage than routine, joyless encounters on autopilot. So take the pressure off. Real intimacy isn't about keeping score it's about staying connected.

Everybody's Doing It... Or Are They?

Here's a jaw-dropper: nearly **60% of married adults** admit to having had at least one affair. That's more than half, folks. While society upholds monogamy as the marital gold standard, many people are privately and sometimes publicly breaking those vows.

This stat doesn't mean marriage is doomed or that humans are hardwired to cheat. But it does highlight the complexities of long-term commitment. Affairs can stem from neglect, emotional disconnection, resentment, or plain old boredom. And while they often bring heartbreak and chaos, they can also spark overdue conversations about unmet needs, dissatisfaction, and what "forever" really entails.

Interestingly, some couples who confront and survive infidelity come out stronger more honest, more self-aware, and clearer on what it takes to maintain trust. Of course, prevention is better than repair. That means being emotionally present, paying attention, and yes keeping the sex life from flatlining. Because let's face it, nobody wants to become the "exception" in their own wedding vows.

Bad Sex Hurts More Than Good Sex Helps

Think one great weekend in bed can fix everything? Think again. Research shows a lack of sex hurts a marriage more than great sex helps it. In other words, no sex creates more dissatisfaction than good sex generates happiness.

Why? Because sexual intimacy is symbolic. It's not just physical it's about feeling desired, valued, and emotionally connected. When that fades, insecurity, distance, and resentment often creep in. It's not that couples need fireworks every time, but they do need to feel like they *want* to be close.

Ironically, trying to fix a dry spell with a "sexy weekend" can backfire if deeper emotional disconnects go unaddressed. Great sex is a bonus. But emotional safety and mutual respect are the foundation.

Even small gestures kisses, touches, long hugs can act as glue. Those tiny moments matter more than you think.

Ancient Wisdom on How Often to "Rejoice"

Even thousands of years ago, couples asked the age-old question: how often should we be doing it? The *Talmud* an ancient Jewish text offered surprising specifics. Idle rich men? Daily. Laborers? Twice a week. Donkey drivers? Once a week. Camel drivers? Once a month. Sailors? Every six months.

Turns out, even 2,000 years ago, people understood that job stress and travel impact intimacy. While it sounds quirky now, this ancient wisdom reflects a timeless truth: sexual frequency is negotiable and context matters.

Modern couples can take a cue. There's no magic number, only mutual understanding. A couple raising toddlers won't match the rhythm of newlyweds or empty-nesters and that's okay. The goal isn't to hit a quota it's to stay connected in a way that works for both of you.

Use It or Lose It (Relationship Edition)

Here's the kicker: couples who engage in regular sexual activity tend to report greater overall marital satisfaction. And no, it's not about porn-level acrobatics it's about intimacy, connection, and shared vulnerability.

Sex is emotional glue. It reinforces the "us" in a relationship, reminding partners they're more than just household co-managers. Physical affection cuddling, spooning, kissing counts, even if it doesn't always lead to sex. These moments keep the emotional temperature warm and the relational bond strong.

The happiest couples say they make intimacy a priority, even if it requires some creativity. Maybe that's scheduling it. Maybe it's hotel getaways, or a "no phones in bed" rule. Maybe it's making out like teenagers while the pasta boils. However it happens the key is to keep it happening

Finale: Bringing the Sizzle Back

Marriage is a marathon, not a sprint. And the truth is, sex in marriage can be complicated, messy, inconsistent and even hilarious. But it can also be deeply fulfilling, beautifully connective, and endlessly evolving. The key isn't constant perfection it's consistent effort.

Keep talking. Keep laughing. Keep touching. And remember: the goal isn't to recapture the heady honeymoon phase forever. It's to build something deeper, more resilient, and yes, still sexy in its own way. Even if that means your hottest night of the week is Tuesday... right after laundry and before the baby monitor goes off.

Spice doesn't have to mean spontaneity 24/7. Sometimes, it's found in the quiet moments, the shared glances, the soft kisses. So go ahead lock the bedroom door. Light a candle, or just turn on the fan.

Keep the flame flickering because even a little glow can light up a marriage.

CHAPTER 4

Meet The In-Laws (And Outlaws): Family, Friends, And the Social Circus

Marriage doesn't happen in a vacuum it happens in the middle of a buzzing beehive of other people. If you thought it was going to be just you, your partner, and a couple of throw pillows from Pottery Barn, think again. In-laws, best friends, coworkers, church folks, neighbors, that one clingy college roommate they all come with the package.

This chapter is your irreverent guide to the expanded cast of characters that can make your marriage feel like a community theater production (charming, if chaotic) or a never-ending episode of *Survivor*.

Let's peel back the curtain and explore seven unexpected, hilarious, and sometimes sobering truths about the social side of marriage. These are the fun facts you wish someone had told you before you said "I do" with 47 people watching and Aunt Marge filming it all on her iPad.

Three's a Crowd (Especially with In-Laws)

Here's the truth: when you marry someone, you marry their family too. It sounds cute on a wedding invitation less so when your mother-in-law critiques your roast chicken or asks pointed questions about your career at Thanksgiving dinner. Studies show 75% of couples experience significant conflict with in-laws. That's three out of four marriages navigating unsolicited opinions, passive-aggressive gifts, or holiday emotional landmines.

Why? Because families are territorial. Marriage shifts family power dynamics, and for some, that shift feels seismic. Suddenly, their baby boy is prioritizing someone else, or their daughter's changing cherished traditions. Cue drama.

Survival tip: Treat in-laws like a second language you don't have to be fluent, but knowing the basics helps. Smile, nod, master the art of vague replies, and above all, back your partner up. Unity is your shield. If your partner doesn't check their parent's behavior, the dirty work falls on you and that rarely ends well.

The Interference Factor: Keep the Peanut Gallery Out

Remember when your parents had "opinions" about your teenage friends? Welcome to the adult remix.

A staggering 81% of happily married couples report minimal interference from friends and family. Compare that with just 38% of unhappy couples who say the same. The math checks out: fewer meddlers, more harmony.

Why is interference so toxic? Because relationships need privacy to grow. Think of it like a garden too many people trampling through, and nothing gets a chance to bloom. Whether it's a best friend who drops by unannounced or a mom narrating your parenting choices, the emotional energy spent managing outsiders leaves less room for nurturing your bond.

How to protect your garden? Boundaries, boundaries, boundaries. Not the brittle kind shouted mid-argument intentional, preemptive ones agreed on and clearly communicated. Maybe no one stays over longer than three nights. Maybe your friend group doesn't get a vote on major decisions. Set the rules early, and you save yourself from emotional weeding later.

Too Close for Comfort: In-Law Friendship Isn't Always a Bonus

Plot Twist: Being Close to Your In-Laws Might Increase Your Risk of Divorce If You're the Wife Research shows that wives who are very close to their in-laws have a 20% higher chance of divorce. In contrast, husbands who maintain strong relationships with their in-laws have a 20% lower chance. What's behind this discrepancy?

It all seems to come down to perception and boundaries. A wife who's close to her in-laws may interpret critical remarks as personal judgments, while a husband might view the same comments as simple advice. It's also about identity. Women often feel judged in their roles as homemakers, mothers, or wives, so what starts as in-law intimacy can shift into scrutiny.

The takeaway? Warm, respectful relationships with in-laws are great, but there's no need to become overly involved. Keep a little distance. Make sure your marriage has room to thrive as its own entity, not as a satellite revolving around someone else's family dynamics.

And ladies, if your mother-in-law wants to become your best friend overnight, it's okay to proceed with caution. You have every right to decline weekly brunches or unsolicited Pinterest boards filled with baby names.

Mixed Faith, Mixed Results

Once upon a time, marrying outside your religion was a headline-worthy event. Now, it's increasingly common. Over 40% of Catholics marry outside their faith, and a similar percentage of American Muslims do the same. Interfaith marriages are reshaping the spiritual and cultural fabric of modern unions.

Enter Chrismukkah, the hybrid holiday celebration where Christmas lights cozy up beside a menorah. Or maybe your family celebrates Eid and Easter in the same month. These marriages can be rich in tradition, empathy, and storytelling, but they also come with challenges navigating different holidays, raising children with dual faiths, or handling disapproval from extended families.

The key to making it work? Communication. Interfaith marriages thrive when both partners are open, respectful, and clear about their expectations. Are you okay with baptizing the baby? Will you fast together during Ramadan? Avoid assumptions and discuss these topics, ideally before your third date, but definitely before buying a joint crockpot.

Faith doesn't have to divide it can deepen your bond, especially if both partners approach it with curiosity rather than defensiveness.

Praying for Patience: Marriage and Religious Participation

Interestingly, Tying the Knot Might Tie You Tighter to Your Faith Married people are nearly twice as likely to attend religious services regularly as singles. Is it spiritual accountability? The need for community? Or perhaps it's the weekly reminder of "thou shalt not kill" during the dishwasher wars?

Whatever the reason, marriage often brings people back to their religious roots. Some find comfort in community support; others seek a moral compass during marital storms. And, sometimes, one partner simply drags the other to service because, well, "we promised Nana."

Don't underestimate the power of shared rituals. Whether it's a Sunday church service, a Shabbat dinner, or lighting candles on anniversaries, these routines add rhythm and meaning. They're not just about belief; they're about belonging.

So, even if you don't consider yourself religious, creating shared rituals spiritual or not can strengthen your partnership. And let's be honest, sometimes marriage does make you pray. For patience. For strength. And for your spouse to put the socks in the hamper.

Born to Be Compatible? Birth Order Matters

It turns out that your place in the sibling lineup may influence your marriage more than your love of rom-coms or your zodiac sign.

Studies suggest that the most successful marriages occur when the oldest daughter of brothers marries the youngest son of sisters. Why? Because of complementary roles. The oldest daughter tends to be nurturing and responsible, while the youngest son is often adaptable and easygoing. It's a match made in sibling-psychology heaven.

On the other hand, marriages between two only children tend to have higher divorce rates. They're used to being the center of attention and may struggle with compromise or sharing emotional bandwidth.

Firstborns married to other firstborns might also clash two natural leaders vying for the captain's chair. Who makes the final decision? Who gets the remote? Who apologizes first? (Spoiler: neither.) Of course, this isn't destiny. Plenty of only-children have wonderful marriages, and many oldest-firstborn pairs find balance. But it's worth considering the dynamics you bring into the relationship. Your childhood role might still be influencing your adult love story.

Trust Over Everything

Let's end with the glue that holds all of this madness together: trust. Surveys consistently show that trust ranks even higher than love, laughter, sex, or forgiveness when it comes to a happy marriage.

Why? Because trust is the foundation. Love might ignite the connection, but trust is what keeps the engine running. You can weather a meddling mother-in-law, a nosy neighbor, or even a crisis of faith, as long as you believe your partner has your back.

Trust isn't just about fidelity. It's about reliability, consistency, and emotional safety. Can you count on them to back you up at a family dinner? Will they keep your secrets? Show up when it matters? Apologize when they mess up? Without trust, every disagreement feels like a threat. Every silence feels like a storm. But with trust, even chaos feels conquerable. You become a team, not two individuals negotiating a treaty.

So, amid the social circus of marriage the friends, the family, the outlaws, and oddballs hold tightly to each other. Learn to laugh through awkward dinners, dance through cultural differences, and build a fortress of trust that outsiders can't shake. Because, in the end, you didn't marry your in-laws, your friends, or the peanut gallery. You married your person. And if the two of you are solid, the rest is just background noise.

Closing Thoughts

Marriage is more than just two people in love. It's two people navigating an entire universe of other humans, traditions, expectations, and unsolicited advice. It's learning to say no (nicely), to choose each other over external noise, and to remember that your relationship is the main event not the sideshow.

So, whether you're dancing around your father-in-law's political rants or celebrating Diwali and Hanukkah in the same week, take heart. Every relationship has its cast of extras. The goal isn't to avoid them, but to keep them from stealing the spotlight.

Now, take a bow. You've earned it.

CHAPTER 5

For Better or For Children – Parenting, Not Parenting, And Marriage

Kids: adorable, exhausting, enlightening, and expensive. They can melt your heart with a sleepy hug and then test your marriage with a temper tantrum in the grocery store. Whether you have them, want them, or actively avoid them, children (or the decision not to have them) fundamentally alter the course of a relationship. In this chapter, Ben and I peel back the curtain on parenting and marriage, exploring the wild ride that comes with adding "Mom" and "Dad" to your titles. From divorce stats tied to daughters to the rising wave of happily childfree couples, these seven facts offer a not-so-filtered look at what really happens when "we" becomes "three" (or four, or five…).

Baby Bliss or Baby Blues? That First Child Can Rock Your Marriage Hard

Let's get this out of the way: babies are cute, but they're also little chaos grenades in footie pajamas. Research shows that a staggering 90% of couples experience a drop in marital satisfaction after the birth of their first child. That's nearly everyone. So, if you've ever sat across from your partner at 2 AM, both bleary-eyed and vaguely hostile, whispering, "What were we thinking?" you're not alone.

The reasons aren't a mystery. Sleep deprivation is torture, literally. Your schedules, priorities, and even your bodies change. Communication often shifts from "How was your day?" to "Did you remember the wipes?" Sex life? You might both rather nap. And somehow, you're supposed to bond through it all. Romantic dinners turn into drive-thru runs. Netflix and chill becomes white noise from the baby monitor, followed by passing out at 8:45.

And yet, we do this. Some of us, multiple times. Why? Because underneath the exhaustion, there's something real shared purpose, love magnified through tiny toes and gummy smiles, and the kind of teamwork that only emerges when you're elbow-deep in diaper blowouts.

But let's be clear: it's okay if you don't love every moment. The perfect parent-couple on Instagram? They're showing you the highlight reel. You're living the full-length documentary.

Pro tip: Make room for grace. Lower the expectations on date nights, your sex life, even the house cleanliness. Trade polished romance for emotional intimacy: "I see you. You're doing your best." That's love too.

Kids as Divorce Insurance Kind Of (But Don't Test This Theory)

You've probably heard couples say they stayed together "for the kids." And, as it turns out, they're not entirely wrong. Statistically, couples with children are slightly less likely to divorce than those without. Kids can act as a kind of social superglue holding couples together even when things aren't exactly sparkling.

There's something about raising a human together that deepens commitment. You see your partner in new ways sometimes frustrating (why can't he remember which sippy cup is the favorite?!), sometimes awe-inspiring (like when she manages bedtime, dinner, and the meltdown over mismatched socks all in one breath). A shared love for your child becomes a daily reminder of why you chose each other in the first place.

But let's not romanticize this too much. Kids can't fix a crumbling relationship, and having a baby to save a marriage is like pouring water on a grease fire and hoping for the best. If anything, kids amplify whatever is already there good or bad. So, if the foundation is shaky, don't count on a stroller to stabilize it.

What kids can do, however, is invite couples to evolve together. If you can grow through parenthood embracing new roles, finding laughter in chaos, and being willing to talk about the tough stuff you might just come out stronger.

Reminder: You're partners, not just co-parents. Keep carving out space to be a couple, even if it's just sneaking in 10 minutes of grown-up talk during naptime.

The 1st Year Parental Crisis: Surviving the "Newborn Nuclear Bomb"

Brace yourself for a blunt statistic: 1 in 5 couples break up within a year of having a baby. That's not a typo. One in five.

The first year of parenthood is often described as a beautiful blur. It's also an emotional minefield. You're dealing with hormone crashes, identity shifts, financial stress, and a total reinvention of your daily life. Communication takes a nosedive. Intimacy often dries up. One or both partners may feel unseen, overburdened, or underappreciated.

Sound familiar? What makes this season especially hard is that most people feel like they're supposed to be happy. If the outside world is saying, "Isn't this the best time of your life?!" but inside you're wondering if you even like your spouse anymore you may feel shame. That shame, if unspoken, becomes a silent wall.

Here's what helps: radical honesty (the kind that says "I'm drowning"), help (family, therapists, sleep consultants take what you can get), and the knowledge that this season will pass.

If you make it through year one intact, celebrate. You've navigated one of the toughest transitions a couple can face. And if you didn't? It doesn't mean you failed. It means you were human.

Note: Don't underestimate the power of small kindnesses. A hot coffee, a thank-you, or a genuine "You're doing a great job" can go a long way when you're both running on empty.

Empty Nest, Full Hearts: Rediscovering Each Other (or Not)

Fast-forward 18 years. The last science project has been turned in. The graduation cap has been tossed. The house is suddenly quiet. You look at your partner and think now what?

It turns out, many couples experience a surge in marital satisfaction once the kids leave home. Without the constant demands of parenting, there's finally time and space to focus on each other again. Spontaneous trips, quiet mornings, revived sex lives (yes, really!), and rediscovered hobbies abound. Some couples even describe it as a "second honeymoon."

But here's the catch: if your marriage was running on autopilot for the sake of the kids, that empty nest can be a rude awakening. All the things you avoided conflicts, distance, mismatched values can resurface with a vengeance.

That's why it's crucial to nurture your relationship throughout the parenting years. Even if it's in small, realistic ways. Talk about more than just the kids. Dream together. Touch base emotionally. Create shared rituals, even if they're as simple as watching your favorite show after bedtime. Because here's the truth: children are a chapter, not the whole story. A strong marriage after kids requires feeding the flame, not just the family.

Encouragement: If you're entering empty nest territory, take it as an invitation not a crisis. Reintroduce yourselves. Travel. Flirt. Make weird late-night snacks. It's your time again.

Ka-Ching! Kids Are Pricey and Money Stress Is Real

We all know kids are expensive. But did you know that raising one child to age 18 in the U.S. costs about $237,000 on average? And that's before college. If your jaw just hit the floor, you're not alone.

From diapers to dance lessons, pediatricians to prom, kids consume more resources than you'd ever expect. And for couples who didn't fully discuss financial expectations before becoming parents, this can quickly become a source of serious strain.

Maybe one parent wants to stay home while the other expects dual incomes. Perhaps someone splurges on every baby gadget while the other is googling "DIY toys made of cardboard." Maybe you both thought you were "savers," but suddenly find yourselves drowning in Amazon Prime boxes.

Money stress is a leading contributor to relationship conflict. Add kids into the mix, and the stakes rise. Financial goals get postponed. Budgets tighten. And if one parent feels financially unsupported or overly burdened resentment can brew.

That's why it's critical to talk money early and often. Not just "Can we afford kids?" but "What kind of lifestyle are we aiming for as a family?" "What values do we want to model about spending and saving?" and yes, "Do we really need that $1,200 stroller?"

Budget tip: Costco, hand-me-downs, and a sense of humor are your best allies. And never underestimate the power of a well-organized secondhand marketplace

Childfree and Happy: The Rise of the "No Kids" Marriage

Let's bust a myth: You don't need children to have a fulfilling marriage. In fact, over 20% of adults are now childfree by choice, and many of them report high levels of life and relationship satisfaction even decades later.

Childfree couples often enjoy more time, more freedom, and more financial flexibility. They can travel spontaneously, pursue ambitious careers, and invest deeply in each other and their communities. Their relationships are often marked by intentionality. They choose this path together, resisting social pressure and forging their own version of happily ever after.

Of course, the pressure is real. "When are you having kids?" can feel like an inescapable refrain at holidays and weddings. Some people assume childfree couples are selfish or "missing out." But those assumptions miss the point. A childfree life isn't a consolation prize. For many, it's the ideal.

Childfree couples also tend to have strong communication, as they've navigated a major life decision together. They've likely talked deeply about values, goals, and long-term plans. That kind of clarity bodes well for relationship health.

If this is you: Ignore the noise. Your joy doesn't need to be justified. Whether you're lounging in a quiet home or adventuring abroad, your love story is valid and valuable.

Daughters vs. Sons: A Strange Divorce Statistic

Ready for a weird one? Studies have found that couples with a firstborn daughter are about 5% more likely to divorce than those with a firstborn son. Even weirder? Couples with three daughters and no sons are up to 10% more likely to split.

Before you panic or accuse your sweet little girl of being a marriage wrecker let's unpack this.

One theory suggests that fathers are more likely to stick around for sons due to gender bonding or social expectations. Another posits that mothers with daughters may feel more supported or empowered to leave unhappy marriages. Still another theory dives into biology: marital stress during pregnancy might slightly increase the odds of female embryos surviving, meaning a daughter could be a symptom of a strained relationship, not the cause.

But here's the real takeaway: correlation is not causation. The presence of daughters doesn't cause divorce. But statistically, it may be associated with marriages that were already on the rocks.

And let's be honest raising girls, especially in a culture that often puts extra pressure on them (and their mothers), can be intense. The emotional depth, the societal expectations, the middle school drama it's a wild ride.

If you're raising daughters, focus on teamwork. Support each other. Communicate. And don't forget to model the kind of love and respect you want your kids to one day seek for themselves

Closing: More Than Mini-Me's

Parenting changes a marriage. Sometimes for the better, sometimes for the bewildering. It can stretch your patience, deepen your love, test your limits, and teach you things about yourself (and your partner) that you never expected.

But it's also not the only path to a meaningful, connected life together. Whether you have kids, want kids, can't have kids, or choose not to, your relationship deserves attention, care, and intention.

So here's the real truth: Kids don't make or break a marriage you do. Your ability to adapt, communicate, laugh, listen, forgive, and show up for each other in whatever family shape you choose is what will write your story.

And if all else fails? There's always therapy, takeout, and the blessed silence of 8 PM bedtime

CHAPTER 6

From "I Do" To "What The?!": Bizarre Marriage Customs & Historical Facts

Let's be real: marriage has never been normal. Sure, today's couples argue over who left dishes in the sink or who forgot to text back. But not too long ago, getting married could involve anything from a kiss that functioned as a legal signature to public shaming if you didn't get hitched fast enough. For centuries, and across cultures, marriage has been less about moonlit walks and more about livestock, legal contracts, and extremely questionable traditions.

This chapter is a wild ride through the weirdest, most fascinating marriage customs and historical facts that would never make it into your Pinterest wedding board. So, whether you're married, single, or still emotionally recovering from your cousin's five-hour wedding in July, grab a drink and settle in because matrimony, it turns out, has always been a little unhinged.

Marriage Was Business, Not Romance (Sorry, Lovebirds)

Pop quiz: What do medieval marriage contracts, feudal alliances, and corporate mergers have in common?

Answer: They all treat relationships like business transactions. Hihihi!

For the vast majority of human history, marriage had nothing to do with love. In fact, if you married for love, people thought you were reckless or just plain foolish. Romantic feelings were nice… but not required. The real goal? Land, livestock, labor, and lineage.

In ancient times, marriage was a way to combine family fortunes, solidify political alliances, or acquire a few extra goats. You didn't marry your soulmate you married the person who came with the right dowry. Royal marriages were often the most extreme example of this, with teenage princesses sent off to marry strangers across borders to prevent wars (or start them). Love was, at best, a side effect. At worst, a liability.

The concept of marrying "for love" didn't really catch on until the late 18th century during the Enlightenment era. Even then, many viewed love as too unstable a foundation for a legal and social institution like marriage. Passion fades, but land holdings? Those stick around.

In a way, this historical context sheds light on modern tensions in marriage. We expect so much from our spouses passion, partnership, parenting skills, friendship, financial stability, and emotional support. No wonder it's hard.

So next time you're annoyed your partner forgot the anniversary, just be grateful they didn't trade you for a plot of land.

Bonus Fact: The term "wedlock" comes from Old English *wed* (a pledge) and *lock* (as in, locked in). Romantic, huh?

Decoy Bridesmaids: Fashion, But Make It Superstitious

Ever wondered why bridesmaids all wear the same dress and why, historically, those dresses looked suspiciously identical to the bride's gown?

Turns out, it wasn't just for the aesthetic. In ancient Rome and later in medieval Europe, bridesmaids were essentially decoys a ghost army of women dressed to confuse vengeful spirits, jealous exes, and the occasional wedding crasher with bad intentions.

The idea was to protect the bride from being targeted. If all the women looked alike, supernatural forces or angry rivals wouldn't know whom to hex, kidnap, or sabotage. Bridesmaids weren't just your closest friends there to toast your new life they were your defense squad. A little like bodyguards in chiffon.

This tradition evolved slowly. By the Victorian era, bridesmaids were still expected to dress similarly to the bride, though now the intent was more symbolic than spiritual. Eventually, color coordination replaced full-on mimicry, leading us to today's endless debates over whether seafoam green or dusty rose looks better in group photos.

So, next time your bestie complains about the satin monstrosity she had to wear, remind her she's continuing a time-honored tradition of being a supernatural decoy. She'll feel slightly better. Maybe.

Bonus Fact: In some cultures, bridesmaids still have protective roles like throwing rice, herbs, or even shoes to ward off bad luck. Fashion with function.

Sealed with a Kiss – A Legally Binding One

"You may now kiss the bride." Today, it's the Instagrammable moment. The swoon-worthy, orchestra-backed climax. But in ancient Rome? That kiss sealed a legally binding contract.

In Roman times, the kiss wasn't just symbolic it was the equivalent of signing a marriage certificate. Contracts, business deals, and treaties were often sealed with a kiss to signify agreement. Marriages were no different. When the couple kissed, the deal was done.

Marriage ceremonies were usually held in front of witnesses, often at the bride's home. After vows were exchanged, the bride and groom kissed cementing the union in the eyes of the law. No kiss? No marriage. (And yes, you can imagine how stressful that might have been for those with performance anxiety.)

Kissing carried a deep symbolic meaning beyond affection. It was a public act of trust and commitment less "I love you," more "I accept the terms and conditions."

Fast forward to today, and while we no longer need the kiss to legalize anything, the tradition stuck. Now it's just a sweet moment… unless Aunt Judy ruins it by standing up for a better camera angle.

Bonus Fact: In medieval Europe, contracts were still "sealed with a kiss." The modern phrase "sealed with a kiss" (SWAK) has ancient legal roots not just mushy romantic ones.

The Oneida Commune: One Big, Weird Marriage

In 1848, in upstate New York, a man named John Humphrey Noyes decided traditional marriage was too restrictive. So, naturally, he founded a religious commune where everyone was married to everyone. Welcome to the Oneida Community, where monogamy was considered selfish and outdated.

This "complex marriage" system meant all men and women were considered spouses. Sex wasn't just encouraged it was seen as a communal responsibility. But not a free-for-all. A committee of elders decided who could sleep with whom, especially when it came to making babies. They even launched a "scientific breeding" program (yes, really), where only select couples were allowed to reproduce, supposedly for eugenic reasons.

Jealousy was discouraged, emotional attachments were monitored, and young boys had to "practice" celibacy to gain control over their desires. Unsurprisingly, this raised more than a few eyebrows and eventually, the community collapsed under the weight of internal drama, external criticism, and Noyes fleeing to Canada.

But here's the weirdest part: After the commune dissolved, some members rebranded themselves as a business and founded Oneida Limited, a successful silverware company still known today.

So next time you eat dinner with Oneida flatware, remember it was born from a 19th-century sex cult. Bon appétit!

Bonus Fact: The Oneida Community operated for over 30 years. Its demise was less due to scandal and more about evolving social norms and leadership disputes.

Forcing the Issue: Get Married or Get Penalized

You think Aunt Lucy asking why you're still single is annoying? Imagine getting fined by the government for not having a spouse.

In ancient civilizations, staying single wasn't just frowned upon it could actually be punishable. For example:

- In Sparta, eligible bachelors were often shamed in public, forced to march naked through the streets or sing humiliating songs.

- Ancient Athens, under the lawmaker Solon, flirted with the idea of making marriage mandatory for adult men.

- The Roman emperor Augustus took it a step further. He imposed the *Lex Julia* and *Lex Papia Poppaea*, laws that penalized singles and rewarded married couples with children. If you were single past a certain age, you could be taxed, denied inheritances, or excluded from political power.

Why the obsession? Simple: Ancient societies needed babies lots of them to sustain economies, fight wars, and carry on the family name. Marriage wasn't a personal choice; it was a civic duty.

Thankfully, today's singles might get guilt-tripped at Thanksgiving, but they won't have their assets stripped at least not unless there's a very bitter breakup involved.

Bonus Fact: Augustus's marriage laws were so strict, even his own daughter was exiled for breaking them. Irony, thy name is Empire.

Til Death (or the River) Do You Part – Babylonian Style

Modern divorce can be messy. But in ancient Babylon, it could be deadly.

The *Code of Hammurabi*, one of the world's oldest legal codes (~1750 B.C.), had very specific rules for marriage and even more brutal rules for divorce. Among them:

- A husband could divorce his wife for failing to bear children, being a "gadabout" (a gossiper or busybody), or neglecting the home.

- If a wife cheated, she could be tied up and thrown into a river. Drowning was considered a form of divine justice if the gods spared her, she was innocent. If not... well, you get the idea.

Meanwhile, if a man cheated? Eh, not nearly as big a deal. (Sense a theme here?)

Marriage was treated as a contract, with women's value largely tied to their fertility and obedience. Violations were met with severe penalties mostly for the woman.

So, yes, modern divorce might involve lawyers, custody battles, and emotional roller coasters but at least no one's throwing anyone into a river.

Bonus Fact: Babylonian marriage contracts were etched in clay tablets and often included clauses about dowries, property rights, and penalties think prenup meets cuneiform

Puritan Punishment: When the Husband Gets Blamed for Cheating

Let's wrap up with a bit of bizarre colonial logic. In 17th-century Massachusetts, one Puritan community had a strange take on marital infidelity: if a wife cheated, her husband got punished too.

The reasoning? If a woman strayed, her husband must have somehow failed in his marital duties physically, emotionally, or spiritually. So, when she was caught, both were thrown into the town stocks, the wooden public punishment device where people sat locked up, often with crowds heckling them.

It was shame, spectacle, and moral lesson all rolled into one. The stocks were usually reserved for petty crimes drunkenness, theft, blasphemy. So, being placed there for your wife's affair? That's insult, injury, and splinters.

This twisted sense of justice reflected deeper ideas about marriage in Puritan society. Wives were seen as morally fragile, and husbands were expected to be their spiritual leaders. If she failed, he must have too.

This archaic blame game didn't last, but it's a striking reminder of how ideas about marriage responsibilities and gender roles have (thankfully) evolved.

Bonus Fact: In some parts of early America, "bundling" (a courtship ritual where a courting couple lay together in bed fully clothed) was encouraged… but only under heavy quilts and family supervision. Because Puritanism = vibes killed.

BONUS CURIOSITIES: Even Weirder Matrimonial Moments

As if the above weren't enough, here are a few more marriage oddities from around the globe and across time:

The Origin of "Bride": Not Romantic

The word "bride" traces back to the Old English word *bryd*, which in turn has linguistic ties to words meaning "to cook." In some cultures, "bride" literally meant "cook." So yes, your ancient role as a wife may have come with a side of meal prep duty.

Italians Smash Stuff (On Purpose)

In Italy, some newlyweds smash glass, dishes, or vases at their reception. The number of broken pieces is said to predict how many years the couple will stay happily married. More shards, more bliss. (Just don't try this with your wedding registry crystal.)

Spit Happens – Especially in Kenya

In the Maasai tribe of Kenya, the father of the bride spits on her head and chest before she leaves to marry. It's a blessing, not an insult though definitely not pandemic-approved.

Bride Kidnapping

In parts of Central Asia, bride kidnapping *ala kachuu* was once practiced (and in some places still occurs). While many modern cases are staged or symbolic, historical bride abduction was very real, and often not consensual. Not exactly the meet-cute we dream of.

Wedding Llamas Are a Thing

In some Andean wedding ceremonies, llamas are dressed up and paraded around as honored guests. They symbolize fertility, wealth, and, presumably, excellent fluffiness.

Final Thoughts: Marriage Still Weird, Still Wonderful

When you look at marriage across time and culture, one thing becomes clear: there's no such thing as "normal." From supernatural bridesmaids to river-bound justice, marriage has been many things legal arrangement, social contract, mystical ritual, moral training ground, and economic tool.

What it hasn't always been is a love story.

Today, as couples around the world redefine what marriage means choosing love over obligation, equality over ownership, and shared values over societal expectations it's fun (and maybe a little sobering) to look back and think: Wow, we've come a long way.

And in some cases, thankfully, we've put down the rope, canceled the river toss, and told the creepy communal cults, "Thanks, but no thanks."

Marriage may never be totally sane but at least we've traded goat dowries for dance floors and public shaming for open bars. Call that progress.

CHAPTER 7

Happily, Never After?: Surprising Facts on Divorce and Aftermath

Ah, divorce. The word itself sounds like a courtroom sigh equal parts legal jargon, emotional gut-punch, and late-night ice cream binge. In this final chapter, we're diving into the topic no one daydreams about when browsing wedding venues: what happens when "forever" ends early. You've read about falling in love, tying the knot, managing in-laws, and laundry schedules. Now let's talk about the part couples never fantasize about but probably should at least think about: what if it doesn't work out?

This chapter isn't here to rain on the wedding parade. It's here to throw a reality-check confetti cannon into the conversation. Because while marriage is full of joy, intimacy, and support, sometimes it turns into silence, sarcasm, or a battle over the dog's vet bills. But if you're going to understand marriage, you also need to understand how and why it ends. So, we're breaking it down: the stats, the causes, the ridiculous court cases, and the weirdly uplifting things that can come after.

Let's talk about eight facts you didn't know you needed until it all goes up in beautifully monogrammed smoke.

The (Not So) Final Countdown: Your Odds Get Worse the More You Try

We've all heard the stat: "Half of marriages end in divorce." But that's like saying, "Half of pizzas are pepperoni." It's oversimplified, somewhat accurate, and leaves out all the juicy details.

Let's dive deeper. According to the Fact Retriever's 2024 data:

- **First marriages** end in divorce about 50% of the time.

- **Second marriages?** A bumpier ride 67% don't make it.

- **Third marriages?** Welcome to the chaos: 74% fail.

That's right. The more you remarry, the worse your odds get. Why? Maybe people bring the same emotional baggage into each new relationship, expecting different results. Or maybe serial spouses just really enjoy wedding cake and courtroom drama.

There's also a psychological element: people who divorce once are more likely to view divorce as a viable escape route. The taboo is gone, the fear is reduced, and sometimes the prenup is better.

If you're thinking of giving marriage another go, you're not doomed but maybe don't treat it like third time's a charm. It's more like a third time's a cautionary tale. Get therapy, get self-aware, and get a really good lawyer (just in case).

Why Splitsville? It's Not Just Cheating and Drama

If you're imagining screaming matches, secret affairs, and someone storming out with a suitcase, slow your soap-opera roll. The real top causes of divorce are far more subtle and arguably more dangerous because of it.

Here's what the Certified Divorce Financial Analyst® (yes, that's a job title) survey found:

- **43% of divorces** are due to basic incompatibility.

- **28%** blame infidelity.

- **22%** cite money issues.

- Abuse, addiction, and other severe problems? Still important but statistically lower.

So, it's not necessarily explosive betrayal that ends marriages. It's the slow erosion of connection. The quiet distance. The "We don't laugh anymore" realization. It's mismatched values, incompatible goals, or one person becoming obsessed with crypto while the other just wants to garden in peace.

Think of it this way: it's not the earthquake, it's the termites.

And that should be both sobering and empowering. It means marriages don't often implode they fade. Which is why ongoing, honest communication is not just a romantic ideal but a lifesaver. Don't let the silence win. Say something before the termites eat the foundation.

'Til Debt Do Us Part: Divorce Costs as Much as the Wedding

Here's a fun irony: The average American wedding costs $20,000–$30,000. And the average divorce? Around $20,000.

Yes, you spend a small fortune to commit and then another one to split. From designer cakes to court filing fees, it's all expensive. You thought the seating chart was stressful? Try negotiating whoever keeps the blender.

The costs include:

- Lawyers (aka the real winners in divorce)
- Mediation fees
- Therapy or counseling (pre- or post-split)
- Moving expenses and new housing
- Division of assets hello, tax accountant bills!

And don't forget the hidden costs: emotional toll, time off work, childcare arrangements, even new furniture. Starting over isn't just emotional it's logistical. It's paperwork, leases, and Target runs for matching dish sets.

Honestly, maybe we need divorce registries. Instead of bath towels and cheese boards, friends can buy you wine, weighted blankets, and IKEA vouchers. There's something beautifully symmetrical about life milestones that both require crockpots.

Petty and Unprecedented: When Divorce Gets Weird

Not every divorce involves dramatic revelations. Some are downright bizarre. Welcome to the corner of human behavior where pasta decisions and passive-aggressive forks become legal matters.

Here are some real-life gems:

- A woman divorced her husband because he served spaghetti instead of turkey on Thanksgiving. She accused him of "culinary neglect" and claimed it endangered their child.

- One man returned home to find his ex-wife had broken in and licked every piece of cutlery out of spite. Stainless steel revenge, anyone?

- Another couple fought over a lottery ticket the wife bought with "shared" funds. The judge ruled the winnings as marital property. Guess who had to share millions with an ex he no longer liked and who hated scratchers?

These tales are hilarious unless you're the one arguing over who gets the pet parrot (true story). But they also highlight something real: divorce brings out the weird. When people feel hurt, they often reach for petty power moves to reclaim control.

Lesson? Keep your dignity. Fight for what matters, not the saltshaker. And maybe hide the silverware.

Divorce Parties: Because Healing Sometimes Needs Cake and Karaoke

Once upon a time, divorce meant shame, stigma, and whispery side-eyes at brunch. Not anymore. Welcome to the age of divorce parties.

Since 1999, divorce celebrations have increased by 22%, and they're only gaining traction. There are now event planners who specialize in uncoupling bashes. Think:

- "Just Divorced!" sashes
- Piñatas shaped like wedding cakes
- Divorce-themed playlists ("I Will Survive," naturally)
- Cakes featuring one figurine pushing the other off the top tier

Some people even go all-out with destination trips, spa weekends, or themed dinners. It's not about mocking the past it's about reclaiming the future. Like a bachelorette party for your next phase.

And let's be real: healing can be messy. There's something cathartic about closing a chapter with friends, music, and cupcakes. After all, you threw a party when you got hitched why not one when you've survived the undoing?

It's not bitterness it's liberation (with frosting).

Life After Love: The Surprising Popularity of Remarrying

Divorce might feel like the end of love, but for many, it's just an intermission. Roughly 60% of divorced individuals remarry, and over 40% of current marriages involve at least one previously divorced partner.

It's human nature we crave connection. Even after heartbreak, betrayal, or years of mismatched life goals, people want to try again. And often, they do it quickly within five years, according to a report from Fact Retriever.

Why? A few reasons:

- • **Emotional optimism**: We're wired to believe in new beginnings.

- • **Familiarity**: Marriage isn't as intimidating the second time some of the mystery is gone.

• **Loneliness**: After a few years of solo pizza nights and Netflix for one, companionship becomes more appealing.

Of course, the statistics remind us that second and third marriages can be riskier. But that doesn't mean they're doomed. The key is learning from the past. Therapy helps. So does dating smarter, not faster. And for some, the sequel really is better than the original.

After all, even Batman got rebooted.

Mind Your Mental (and Physical) Health

Here's the part people don't talk about enough: divorce affects your body. Divorce is ranked just below the death of a spouse on the Holmes and Rahe Stress Scale, meaning it can:

- **Weaken your immune system**
- **Raise blood pressure**
- **Disrupt sleep**
- **Lead to depression or anxiety**

In short, it's not just a breakup it's a biological event.

And here's the twist: being in a toxic marriage can be even worse for your health than divorce. Chronic conflict raises cortisol, inflames the body, and chips away at long-term health. So, if you're staying "for the kids," remember that what kids need most is not two parents who just happen to stay together but two healthy ones.

If you're going through a split, don't just lawyer up **self-care up**. Consider:

- Therapy (individual, not just couples)

- **Group support or divorce meetups**
- **Physical activity (rage-walking counts)**
- **Taking a break from dating**

Post-divorce healing isn't just about moving on it's about moving inward. Don't grit your teeth and power through. Tend to your emotional wounds as you would a broken bone.

Still Worth It: Why Marriage Continues to Matter

Okay, after all this divorce drama, you might be wondering why do people even get married anymore? Isn't it just legal paperwork wrapped in emotional risk?

Well, maybe. But also **no**.

According to a 2024 study, marriage still contributes more to long-term life satisfaction than money, sex, or children. Yep, when it's good, marriage is really good.

Marriage offers:

- Deep companionship
- A reliable emotional anchor
- A sense of shared purpose
- Social and financial benefits

Of course, a bad marriage can do the opposite. But that's like saying a terrible vacation means travel is always awful. The real question is how you travel and who you travel with.

Good marriages are built, not stumbled into. They require emotional intelligence, conflict-resolution skills, and a willingness to grow together. And if you're willing to do the work, the rewards are real.

So, is it worth it? That depends. But for many, even with all the risk, heartache, and late-night fights over thermostats, the answer is still **yes**.

Marriage isn't a fairy tale. It's more like a road trip amazing with the right person, miserable with the wrong one, and always unpredictable.

Final Optimistic Notes: Divorce Is an Ending, Not the Ending

We tend to treat divorce as failure. But maybe we should rethink that.

Sometimes, divorce is growth. It's two people acknowledging that the contract they signed no longer fits the people they've become. It's brave. It's painful. And it's often necessary.

Marriage is a beautiful gamble. And divorce? It's the moment you decide to fold hopefully with grace, maturity, and the promise to play again, smarter.

Whether you're newlywed, long-wed, remarried, or happily single, this chapter (and this book) wasn't meant to scare you it was meant to prepare you. Love is complicated. Commitment is hard. But with humor, honesty, and self-awareness, you can navigate it all.

So here's to love in all its forms, in all its chaos, and even in its endings.

Now, go eat cake. Married, divorced, or dating your cat everyone deserves frosting

Till Debt Do Us Part: The Real Cost of Marriage (And Divorce)

As Emma sat on her couch, staring at the pile of unopened bills on her coffee table, she couldn't help but wonder how things had come to this. She and Dave had been college sweethearts, full of dreams and plans. But here they were, years later, arguing over every cent spent and who owed whom. Their wedding day felt like a distant memory an extravagant affair everyone admired, but one that had also set them back more than they cared to admit.

They used to laugh at each other's silly financial habits, like Dave's obsession with top-shelf whiskey or Emma's penchant for pricey home décor. Now, those quirks had snowballed into arguments, with neither able to see eye to eye on what once seemed trivial.

The reality is money can silently erode even the strongest bonds if not managed wisely. From overly ambitious wedding budgets to mysterious "financial infidelities," dealing with finances in a relationship isn't just awkward it's essential. This chapter takes a closer look at how love and money intertwine not always in perfect harmony and how these dynamics shape the foundation of both flourishing marriages and tumultuous splits. Let's dive into the world where romantic dreams collide with the stark reality of dollars and cents.

Wedding Wallet Woes

The cost of a wedding can make anyone shudder or perhaps laugh, depending on which side of the aisle you're sitting. In some places, it's all about the grand showcase. The average American wedding, for example, hovers around $30,000. Cross over to India, and you'll find magnificent affairs, the kind Bollywood dreams are made of, often costing less due to local purchasing power and familial support. In Venezuela, amid economic challenges, couples still aim for a fairy tale wedding, using clever, budget-friendly alternatives to keep love alive without breaking the bank.

Differences in wedding spending reflect not only economic status but also cultural values. Japan's weddings, transcending monetary logic, often feature gifts like the ceremonial sake barrel, which symbolizes prosperity a tradition difficult to put a price tag on. In Italy, the focus shifts from splurging on extravagant venues to serving culinary delights; after all, nothing says celebration like a five-course meal, right?

Some eye-popping expenses stem from much deeper cultural roots. Consider the Filipino custom of the money dance, where guests pin bills directly onto the happy couple's attire. The spectacle not only provides financial support but also offers a family-centered take on wedding rituals. In South Africa, lobola negotiations involve bargaining over the bride price a norm rooted in cultural values and respect, even if it sounds outlandish to some.

Yet, it's the peculiarities that truly spice up the financial picture. For instance, the cake isn't just a cake; it's a reflection of the couple's love story. In the USA, a four-tiered, intricately designed wedding cake can cost as much as a small car. Or imagine a Caribbean wedding where guests exchange vows underwater, with the price tag covering not just bouquets but also scuba gear. In the UK, one couple even brought goats as ring bearers' humor and potential mischief included, at no extra cost.

Cultural or emotional ties often guide these decisions. In China, the number of bridesmaids is not just about best friends but also about showcasing social networks, extending beyond mere expense. Across cultures, you'll find anecdotes of pineapple centerpieces, fireworks replacing confetti, or even those who decide to marry in zero gravity a fantasy beyond most earthbound wallets' reach. While peculiar, these choices symbolize personal bonds rather than financial acumen.

Let's not forget the attire. The wedding dress remains a powerful symbol whether it's adorned with crystals, colored red for luck, or custom-designed to avoid any horror-movie bride mishaps. In the UK, grooms may wear traditional Scottish kilts, adding heritage to each thread. Veils, long trains, and intricate lace can rack up costs, especially when paired with rare flowers and silk bridesmaid ensembles.

Often, the most pressing question is: who pays these skyrocketing sums? In many Eastern cultures, the groom's family typically bears the financial burden, linking back to values of commitment and respect. In Western contexts, expenses are split more evenly or fall to the couple themselves, reflecting modern views on financial independence.

From elephants replacing limousines in Indian weddings to five-course feasts worthy of Michelin stars in France, wedding spending reflects choices that may baffle some and delight others. As the cost meter ticks upward, considerations often shift from practicality to symbolic gestures underscoring a lifelong bond or at least lasting impressions on Instagram.

In this dance between finance and fantasy, weddings can teach valuable lessons in budgeting. Before diving into the bliss of matrimony, it's worth pausing to smile at the peculiarities that challenge norms. Enterprising couples can find ways to maintain fiscal prudence without sacrificing dreams. Custom ice sculptures and personalized vows over the South Pole sit side by side with intimate backyard ceremonies all differing in cost, yet equally bonded by the celebration of love.

Ultimately, the intertwining of finance and relationships offers a sneak peek into the frazzled discussions that might follow when one partner discovers a passion for high-end coffee tables, while the other is perfecting DIY decor from scratch. Navigating these dynamics lays the groundwork for tougher conversations down the line.

As we shift focus to who picks up the tab, it's more than just a cultural difference; it's an exploration of family politics and evolving expectations. This shift may provoke introspection: in a world where romance meets finance, who truly bears the expense?

Wedding Wallet Woes

Considering global wedding costs sheds light on how couples often empty their bank accounts for traditions that span mere hours. A Swedish bride might emerge from a month-long whirlwind of appointments, her gown worth a significant chunk of her savings, while across the world, an Indian groom's family showers splendor in multi-day festivities. Navigating these expenses unveils a bouquet of cultural expectations and unspoken financial rules. The question of who pays for it all can become as intricate as the ceremonial details themselves.

Traditionally, in Western contexts, the bride's father typically took on this role, a centuries-old practice symbolizing the family's willingness to offer their daughter's hand. This gesture often left parents viewing their nest eggs as little more than wedding dowries. In contrast, Middle Eastern customs designate the groom's family as the financiers. This isn't just out of generosity but as a testament to the groom's ability to provide a critical barometer for his suitability. These cultural roles can clash with modern attitudes about financial independence, where dual-income couples split costs to reflect shared life goals.

Yet, peek beneath the surface of these traditional institutions, and you'll uncover contemporary shifts, driven by economic pressures and social evolution. In China, lavish weddings still signal status, with families spending large portions of their annual income on extravagant ceremonies. However, rapid urbanization and rising costs have led many couples to opt for city registry offices, prioritizing practicality over opulence. It's an increasingly common theme: modern couples navigating wedding costs with one foot firmly planted in tradition and the other firmly in the world of practicality.

Traveling across the Atlantic to Brazil, couples face their own set of challenges. Weddings are massive social events, often involving hundreds of guests. Families tend to share costs more evenly, but the process is far from simple. Every decision from floral arrangements to reception venues becomes a line item for negotiation. Who pays for what often hinges more on family dynamics than cultural customs? Parents who argue over wedding expenses may inadvertently pass unresolved familial tensions onto the couple, potentially straining future relationships.

Dynamics in Japan

can look quite different, where couples often bear a significant portion of the wedding costs. This shift reflects broader trends, such as late marriages and greater independence before tying the knot. While Japanese families honor tradition through kimonos and ancient rituals, financial support is more often reserved for pressing matters like homeownership. In this environment, couples navigate a delicate balancing act, striving to honor family while staying true to their financial aspirations.

In the Western world, wedding planning has evolved into a complex financial endeavor. Checklists and pivot tables now rival love letters and poems. Even as couples increasingly share expenses, the hefty price tags for venues, photographers, and caterers can spark tense conversations. The question of who should pay for what often becomes a dance each step feels more like a negotiation than a smooth glide toward marital bliss.

In **Nigeria**, the Ebira people celebrate elaborate weddings where family contributions are not just expected but eagerly anticipated. Here, communal involvement underscores deep familial ties, and a family's societal standing is often measured by the wedding they present. These traditions not only establish expectations but also bind communities together, symbolizing both financial and emotional support for the newlyweds.

Similarly, **India** often depicted through the lens of colorful, grand celebrations hosts intense cultural debates over wedding costs. Families extend lavish hospitality, blending economic reality with cultural pride. In regions where arranged marriages are still common, wedding planning often becomes a logistical marathon, where financial considerations and customs collide. However, the influence of urbanization is driving change, encouraging couples to prioritize personal choice and partnership over parental financial support.

The evolving narrative across these diverse cultures reveals that couples are no longer bound by tradition alone; they innovate, negotiate, and occasionally challenge the practices of previous generations. In these love stories, budgeting becomes an essential part of the equation, merging respect for tradition with modern financial realities.

Financial transparency

is now a vital part of marriage planning, as essential as florists and catering contracts. As money begins to flow through the tapestry of a relationship, open discussions about finances can become an ally rather than an adversary. These conversations help couples navigate potential financial challenges with honesty, potentially laying the foundation for marital harmony. Concepts like "financial therapy" are emerging not as luxuries but as necessities designed to foster integrity and ensure stability in relationships. When we discuss financial therapy, we're not just managing money; we're managing relationships.

In the subsequent paragraphs, we'll explore how couples who regularly discuss their finances experience greater relationship satisfaction. Understanding how money intersects with personal values and long-term dreams becomes critical. Budgeting evolves into a love language one not expressed in cash, but in the shared commitment to understanding and improving future goals. This focus on financial health can form the bedrock of relationship success, providing a glimpse into the golden marriages where openness and financial harmony prevail.

Financial Red Flags in Marriage

In different cultures, financing a wedding can be a significant concern. Who pays for what from the bride's dress to the venue can vary widely. However, beneath these traditions lies a common thread: the importance of financial transparency in marriage. How couples handle wedding finances often sets the tone for future financial discussions. Addressing expectations early on creates a foundation of openness and understanding in a marriage.

This transparency extends beyond the wedding day. A fun fact worth noting: Couples who engage in weekly discussions about money report higher levels of happiness. Why is that? Regular financial dialogue fosters financial intimacy. It's about collaborating on a shared vision for the future. For example, some couples turn their financial check-ins into a ritual. Picture them sitting down every Sunday evening, perhaps over a cup of tea, to review the week's expenditures and plan for upcoming expenses. These seemingly mundane conversations elevate everyday intimacy, fostering collaboration over conflict.

Beyond routine discussions, another innovative tool gaining traction is **financial therapy**. This isn't just for couples facing financial distress; it's for anyone wanting to improve their understanding and management of money matters. Financial therapy combines elements of financial planning and relationship counseling. Imagine sitting with a financial therapist, reviewing your financial statements, discussing goals, and delving into your emotional responses to money issues. For instance, consider a couple who argue over discretionary spending. Through therapy, they might discover that one partner views spending as a treat, while the other sees it as wasteful. Recognizing these underlying beliefs helps to prevent potential conflicts.

Success stories from financial therapy highlight its value. One couple discovered that one partner's anxiety around finances stemmed from childhood experiences of scarcity. Another couple learned to view financial planning as a team-building exercise, transforming a potentially divisive task into a bonding ritual. These examples show how financial therapy not only resolves current disputes but strengthens the relationship's foundation.

Couples across the spectrum approach financial matters creatively. Some adopt the "Yours, Mine, and Ours" budget. In this approach, a portion of income is allocated for individual discretionary spending, while the rest is directed toward shared goals. This strategy respects personal autonomy while maintaining collective responsibility. For example, one couple set up separate accounts for personal expenditures, reducing friction around spending. As the saying goes, less scrutiny sometimes leads to more harmony.

Others take a different approach, implementing a monthly 'money night.' These check-ins are not just for staying on top of finances but also serve as a playful date night activity. Couples pair their financial discussions with dinner or a board game, making the process more enjoyable. Reinventing financial conversations into something fun shifts the focus from problem-solving to partnership-building.

In essence, these strategies and tools act as pillars of financial stability in a relationship. They don't merely avert potential disputes they cultivate an environment where financial decisions are shared responsibilities. Couples who embrace financial transparency from the start often find that it forms the bedrock of their relationship, fostering a healthier, happier union.

However, ignoring financial issues can lead to significant problems. Financial stress can seep into every aspect of life, including intimacy. As we transition into exploring the profound connection between credit scores and sex lives, it becomes clear that financial stability or lack thereof not only impacts our bank accounts but our bedrooms as well. The way financial stress translates into emotional distance and its impact on relationships will be examined further, shedding light on money-related issues as key predictors of divorce.

Financial Red Flags: Debt Issues

In previous discussions, we've explored the importance of regular financial communication in relationships. Couples who engage in open conversations about money tend to experience higher levels of happiness. We've also seen the rise of "financial therapy," which is helping couples navigate these tricky conversations effectively. But how do credit scores tie into these discussions, and what unexpected consequences can they have on our relationships? Let's explore.

When we think about credit scores, they may seem like just a number something of interest to banks, not bedrooms. However, here's where it gets interesting: Social scientists have found that credit scores can provide valuable insights into relationship success. While love may last forever, credit can change with a single financial misstep. This is exactly why credit scores should not be overlooked when considering relationship dynamics.

Imagine this scenario: Two people, deeply in love, but with vastly different financial histories. One partner has a pristine credit score, easy access to loans, and enjoys a low-interest financial world. The other, on the other hand, has struggled with managing finances, and their credit score tells that story. Now, the question arises: Does this financial mismatch matter as much as whether pineapple belongs on a pizza?

Research says yes. A significant difference in credit scores can predict conflicts and even unhappiness in a marriage. These scores have an uncanny ability to forecast marital success or failure almost as accurately as a horoscope. When one partner consistently struggles with financial issues, the stress doesn't just impact the bank account it seeps into the relationship, creating tension and potentially leading to altercations and mistrust.

Money disagreements become a recurring theme. Financial compatibility or lack thereof can be a major predictor of divorce. While we all know money talks, in this case, it's shouting, "You're not financially compatible!" It may sound harsh, but this is a reality that many couples face without realizing it. We've seen couples with mismatched financial habits from the start, torn apart by money issues, even when their emotional connection seemed solid.

For some, it's not just about the obvious red flags like bankruptcy or missed payments. It's about the deeper implications money has on everyday life. Take, for example, the couple next door, who, after moving in together, discovered that their differing financial habits created more friction than the crumbling kitchen. The stress of managing shared expenses finally surfaced during a heart-to-heart conversation, which quickly turned into an argument about finances. This snowballed, ultimately affecting their intimacy. Over time, these seemingly small financial irritations grew into a major wedge or, more accurately, a chasm.

Imagine this scenario: You come home after a long day, excited about a surprise date night. But then you discover an unexpectedly high credit card bill on the counter. Suddenly, the fantasy of a romantic evening is replaced by a not-so-romantic discussion. If these moments aren't navigated with understanding and empathy, they can lead to frequent disputes, slowly eroding intimacy like a series of small financial paper cuts.

But financial awareness isn't just about avoiding another argument over that surprise credit card bill. It's about understanding the financial landscape before you set foot on shared financial ground. Awareness can help you avoid painful surprises down the road. Here's a dare: The next time you have one of these "discussions," try complimenting your partner on their financial literacy. The response might surprise you!

Let's inject a little humor into this otherwise serious topic. Think of financial therapy as yoga for your wallet: stretch, breathe, and bend toward a better financial future together. This approach doesn't just realign conversations about spending habits, savings, and credit card usage it also opens the door to more fulfilling intimacy. When handled with care, these discussions can evolve from financially-focused quarrels to harmonious financial Zen.

Our journey through the intersection of finances and relationships isn't over. With financial disagreements being a key predictor of divorce, it's clear that financial fitness deserves equal importance to emotional or physical attraction in a relationship. A healthy relationship, much like a healthy body, requires balance, and that includes financial balance.

As we wrap up this segment, let's take a peek at what's next: Untangling the fascinating cases of couples who've parted ways over cryptocurrency yes, Bitcoin and its digital cousins have caused their fair share of separations! We'll dive into how disputes over digital assets have shaken up marriages, resulting in evolving statistics on alimony, settlements, and asset divisions. Stay tuned, because while cryptocurrency might seem abstract, its impact on modern marriages is as tangible as a platinum wedding band.

By keeping these conversations alive, we ensure that financial literacy becomes a shared adventure, not a battlefield. Make time for these discussions, so that, unlike the couple from earlier, you recognize that financial love languages can be just as vital to discuss as your favorite Netflix series to binge-watch together

Debt and Divorce; The Prenup Boom

Credit scores might seem like just numbers on a report, but they hold more power in relationships than you might think. There's a fascinating link between having similar credit scores and smoother relationships. Couples with closely aligned scores tend to argue less, suggesting that financial compatibility goes beyond just the digits. It's about shared financial habits and outlooks that foster intimacy and understanding. Money issues, a top predictor of divorce, don't just stem from an empty bank account they're often rooted in deeper issues like trust and transparency that unravel relationships.

Now, let's shift gears to some unexpected financial topics that might not make it onto a marriage checklist, but definitely impact how that journey unfolds.

Take cryptocurrency, for instance. Usually parked under tech and finance, it's rarely considered when discussing marital compatibility. Yet, it's emerging as a modern-day financial wedge for some couples. In certain cases, partners struggle to reconcile the risk-taking behavior that crypto investments demand. Digital coins aren't tangible, and their abstract nature can breed distrust especially when one partner dives into crypto without consulting the other. Cryptocurrency becomes a symbol for larger relationship issues, like control and communication, which go beyond the financial.

Then, there's the evolving landscape of prenups. Once seen as unromantic, prenuptial agreements are now firmly on the table, especially among younger generations. Millennials and Gen Z aren't just outlining asset divisions; they're getting creative with clauses that reflect modern lifestyles. Think pet custody arrangements or rules governing social media behavior post-split. Imagine sitting down with your partner and deciding who gets the Instagram handle for your beloved dog or agreeing not to post disparaging comments online after a breakup. These types of arrangements underscore how deeply our digital lives have intertwined with our personal lives.

On a lighter note, celebrity prenups can be downright entertaining. They offer a fascinating blend of cautionary tales and extravagant financial foresight. The jaw-dropping demands and clauses of some Hollywood stars sometimes read more like movie scripts. These documents not only protect assets but also showcase evolving relationship norms and the unique expectations couples have for each other financially. In many ways, these extravagant clauses highlight the lengths to which the wealthy and famous go to plan for the possibility of a split even before they say, "I do."

Let's not forget **alimony** and the statistical snapshots that reflect evolving societal norms. Did you know nearly half of married couples may experience divorce? In that light, alimony isn't just a legal term echoing in courtrooms it has real, practical implications in many lives.

Take, for example, the newer trend of *rehabilitative alimony*, where payments are intended to help a lower-earning partner regain financial independence rather than provide indefinite support. It's a modern approach that acknowledges shifting roles within marriages and promotes self-sufficiency.

Equally telling are the statistics around asset division particularly when it comes to home ownership. For many, the family home symbolizes security and stability. Yet, in divorce proceedings, it often becomes a contentious issue, disproportionately affecting women who may have invested more time and care into the home than their names on deeds might reflect.

Now, let's swing back to *prenups* and touch on another emerging phenomenon: **prenup parties**. Yes, they're real and surprisingly festive. On the surface, they may seem paradoxical, but they align with a growing cultural shift toward financial transparency in relationships. These gatherings aren't just about signing contracts they're about destigmatizing money talk and turning what was once considered taboo into a celebration of honesty. Guests, usually close friends and family, gather in support, and there's often genuine revelry, transforming an otherwise legal formality into a shared, empowering moment.

As we reflect on these evolving dynamics, one theme becomes clear: **money**, in all its forms, is deeply and inextricably woven into the fabric of both marriage and divorce. From the buzz (or dread) around cryptocurrencies to the legally binding terms of a prenup and even the normalization of discussing finances at a party our romantic partnerships are shaped, sustained, and sometimes strained by economics.

While love may feel immeasurable and eternal, the infrastructure around it is built on quantifiable, often rigid numbers. Learning to balance these numbers like we balance expectations, dreams, and disappointments becomes both an art and a skill, and, at times, a source of conflict. Much like the relationships themselves.

So, as we navigate the turbulent waters of marriage and money, perhaps the most valuable takeaway is this: **transparency is a shield**. Trust, fortified by open and honest conversations about financial matters, builds not only a foundation for lasting love but also a firewall for the inevitable challenges that arise. When we strip away the taboos and embrace financial clarity, we reinforce the very bonds that connect us whether we're counting pennies or bitcoins

Bringing It All Together

As we've journeyed through the fascinating maze of wedding finances, one thing is certain; while love may be priceless, weddings most definitely are not. Understanding how money intricately weaves itself into marital bliss or chaos offers valuable insights for anyone preparing to tie the knot. But here's the good news: armed with this knowledge, couples can now approach financial discussions with humor and openness, transforming potential pitfalls into opportunities for growth. By embracing the absurdities and leaning into financial transparency, couples can build marriages rooted in honesty and resilience. So, as you step forward, remember while your wedding may be just one day, your financial partnership is for life. Let's make it both enjoyable and enduring!

CHAPTER 9

Where To Go: Travel, Living, And Escaping the In-Laws

Married life often means merging two households, two families, and sometimes two very different ideas of "home." This chapter explores domestic adventures, family drama, and funny facts about couple living arrangements.

Love and Location

"Love may be blind, but it still needs good Wi-Fi and a decent school district."

When you first fall in love, you don't ask deep, important questions like, "Do you snore like a tractor in winter?" or "Would you ever consider living somewhere without indoor plumbing?" No. You talk about dreams, shared playlists, and whether pineapple belongs on pizza. (It doesn't. Don't @ us.)

But once marriage enters the chat, so does real estate. Suddenly, the most romantic phrase you can hear isn't "I love you," but "I found a place with a dishwasher and no HOA fees."

The Most Romantic (and Most Stressful) Places to Live as a Couple

Let's start with some locations that practically drip with romantic possibility:

- **Paris:** Croissants, kisses, and charming apartments the size of a closet.

- **Venice:** Gondola rides, wine, and a mold problem no amount of bleach can solve.

- **Bali:** Beautiful sunsets, cheap massages, and at least one monkey that will steal your sunglasses and your dignity.

But for every swoon-worthy city, there's the "Oh no, we actually live here now" realization:

- **New York:** Romantic rooftop views if you can afford one. Otherwise, it's "romantic" fourth-floor walkups and rats with attitude.

- **San Francisco:** Great weather, if you enjoy fog and paying $3,000 for a closet with a view of a dumpster.

- **Any Suburb:** Affordable, but you may have to sacrifice your soul to HOA meetings and lawn politics.

Why Moving in Together Doesn't Always Save Money

Spoiler alert: *Love doesn't automatically come with financial savings.*

Sure, in theory, splitting the rent or mortgage should be economical. But in reality, couples often find themselves locked in mortal combat over whether the thermostat should stay at 72 degrees or be set to "Arctic Tundra."

Here are some sneaky costs that come with cohabitation:

- The "Joint Decor" Debacle: That reclaimed wood coffee table she loves? $500. The therapy you need after assembling it together? Priceless.

- Grocery Inflation: Two people eat more than one. Shocking.

- The "His and Hers Streaming Services" Dilemma: Because one simply cannot survive on just Netflix.

The Phenomenon of "Living Apart Together" Marriages

Welcome to modern love: where you're married, deeply committed, and… live in different houses.

The "Living Apart Together" (LAT) lifestyle is trending among couples who value both intimacy and individual closet space. These couples argue less about toothpaste tubes and more about which city to rendezvous in for the weekend.

Perks include:

- **Personal space.**
- **Better appreciation for time together.**
- **No passive-aggressive fights about whether the laundry should be folded "your way" or "the correct way."**

In other words: some couples have cracked the code. Live together emotionally, apart spatially.

In-Laws, Outlaws, and Social Landmines

"You marry the person, but you also marry their mother's opinion on how you cook chicken."

Ah yes, the in-laws. Those mysterious beings who gave your spouse life and now want to give *you* unsolicited advice on everything from diaper cream to dining chairs. In-law dynamics are a universal marital challenge. In fact…

Fun Fact: 60% of Couples Report In-Law Drama as a Source of Tension

That's right. More than half of married couples admit that dealing with their partner's family causes stress. The other 40% are either lying or live on a different continent.

Here are the **Top In-Law Complaints** (from both sides):

- **From Spouses:** "She calls every day. Multiple times. And texts pictures of casseroles."

- **From In-Laws:** "We're just trying to help. And also redecorate your entire living room while you're at work."
- **From Both:** "He still lets his mom do his laundry. At 34."

Real-Life Tales of In-Law Overstep (And How Couples Managed It)

Let's meet a few brave souls who've been in the trenches:

- **The Thermostat Tyrant:** Jenny's mother-in-law would reset the thermostat *every time* she visited. Solution? They installed a fake second thermostat. Mother-in-law felt in control. Jenny stayed warm. Win-win.

- **The Pop-In Parents:** Dave's in-laws had a spare key and zero boundaries. They once "surprised" the couple during date night. Dave changed the locks and told them it was due to a "security update." He wasn't wrong.

- **The Name Game:** Priya's father-in-law refused to call her by her actual name, instead calling her "Prema" (his ex-girlfriend's name) for the first six months. Eventually, Priya started responding in Latin. He got the message.

Solutions vary. Sometimes it's therapy. Sometimes it's tequila. Often, it's setting boundaries so sharp you could slice a fruitcake on them.

Travel: Bonding or Breaking Point?

"Nothing tests a marriage like trying to find Wi-Fi in a foreign country while you're both hangry and sunburned."

Couples often imagine travel as this dreamy, Instagrammable adventure. But behind every cute photo of matching sunhats is a deeply unspoken truth:

One of you is lost. The other is pretending not to be angry about it.

Do Couples Who Road Trip Together Stay Together?

They just might if they can survive the Great GPS Debate of 2023. Or if they don't murder each other over playlist control. Or if someone (not naming names, Brian) doesn't insist on taking "the scenic route" that adds three hours and a flat tire to the journey.

Still, road trips can reveal key relationship truths:

- **Who's the control freak?**
- **Who can't pack light?**
- **Who will crack first when the hotel only has decaf.**

"Vacation Divorces" – How Travel Can Make or Break a Marriage

You've heard of destination weddings. Now meet their evil twin: **vacation divorces.**

It's a real thing. Some couples travel together and return... single.

Why?

- **Expectations vs. Reality:** You imagined slow walks on the beach. You got heat rash and food poisoning.
- **Different Travel Styles:** One person wants to hike. The other wants to nap. Forever.
- **24/7 Together Time:** Love may be eternal, but that doesn't mean you need to spend *every* second together. Even Romeo and Juliet had alone time (albeit tragically short).

Hilarious Honeymoon Mishaps from Around the Globe

- **Thailand:** A newlywed couple accidentally joined a yoga retreat instead of a beach resort. Let's just say their "downward dog" wasn't part of the plan.

- **Italy:** One husband tried to surprise his wife by renting a Vespa. He forgot he didn't know how to ride it. The Vespa made it three blocks. Their marriage made it through the ER.

- **Costa Rica:** A romantic treehouse stay turned into a monkey invasion at 3AM. Nature: 1, Romance: 0.

Travel builds character. And sometimes, character builds bail money.

Home Is Where the Chaos Is

"They say love builds a home, but no one mentions the IKEA hex key required."

Once you're back from your emotionally fraught honeymoon, it's time to settle into home life. Which means negotiating everything from laundry schedules to whether "shoes-off" is a lifestyle or a war cry.

Division of Chores and the "Chore Gap" Debate

Ah yes, the age-old conflict: who does what, how often, and why hasn't it been done yet?

Common scenarios:

- **The Passive-Aggressive Post-It:** "If the dishes magically clean themselves, please share the spell."

- **The 'Weaponized Incompetence' Defense:** "I just don't do it as well as you do, honey."

- **The 'But I Mow the Lawn!' Argument:** Used as a blanket excuse for not vacuuming since 2009.

Studies show that unequal division of chores is a leading source of resentment. But if both partners agree on a system or agree to outsource peace is possible.

Just don't expect applause for unloading the dishwasher. That's not "helping." That's just being a functioning adult.

Bizarre Cohabitation Contracts

Some couples are taking no chances. They're drawing up cohabitation agreements with clauses like:

• "No talking before coffee."

. "All thermostat disputes shall be settled via rock-paper-scissors."

. "Decor purchases over $100 require unanimous approval *and* a Pinterest board."

One legendary contract from a Reddit couple even included:

"Under no circumstances will extended family be allowed to sleep over without 72-hour notice and emotional preparation."

We salute them.

Home Decor Fights and Furniture Wars (IKEA Strikes Again!)

If you've never argued about a couch, are you even married? Home decor is where personal taste and tension collide.

It's also where many couples first discover:

■ One of you is a minimalist.

■ The other collects vintage 1950s ashtrays like they're rare gems.

And then... there's IKEA the ultimate relationship crucible.

You may enter the store holding hands, dreaming of open shelving and Swedish meatballs. But by the time you're assembling the MALM dresser with 73 screws and a hex wrench shaped like regret, you're seriously questioning your life choices.

Some couples make it through. Others walk away and live forever among unpacked boxes.

Finale: Domestic Bliss or Battlefield?

Marriage is a journey sometimes to another city, sometimes just to the other side of the bed. Whether you're navigating in-laws who treat boundaries like suggestions, surviving travel disasters with your dignity (mostly) intact, or negotiating who's responsible for cleaning the shower grout (spoiler: no one wants that job), remember:

Love isn't about never fighting. It's about learning to fight fair, laugh through the chaos, and maybe just maybe agree on a wall color.

And if all else fails? There's always the guest room at your parents' house. Just... maybe don't tell your in-laws you're staying there.

CHAPTER 10

How To Move on: Divorce, Dating Again, And Fun Facts from The Other Side

Theme: This chapter lightens the mood around breakups, showing that divorce isn't just an end it can be a hilarious, enlightening, and even empowering new beginning. Let's toast to freedom cakes, swipe rights, and glow-ups that make your ex say, "Wait, what happened to *them*?!"

Breaking Up Is Hard to Do... But Also Kinda Funny

Ah, divorce. The word alone sounds like a courtroom drama with a side of wine-soaked tears and awkward legal jargon. But once you peel away the clichés, you'll find that divorce isn't just sad it can be absurd, weird, and downright hilarious.

The Oddest Reasons Cited in Divorce Filings

Forget infidelity or "irreconcilable differences." Real-life couples have parted ways for reasons that make reality TV look boring. Behold, some *actual* reasons cited in divorce filings:

- **"She had a secret affair... with the dishwasher."** One husband claimed his wife's unhealthy obsession with loading the dishwasher "wrong" was grounds for divorce. Every time he stacked a plate; she'd rearrange it with the intensity of a bomb technician.

- **"My wife was possessed by a ghost."** A man in New York asked for a divorce because he said his wife "refused to stop being haunted." She insisted the spirit was friendly. He disagreed. So did the judge.

- **"He brought his mother on our honeymoon."** This one needs no explanation except to say the mother-in-law also insisted on sleeping between the couple "for comfort."
- **"She constantly spoke in Klingon."** A man claimed his wife's immersion in Star Trek cosplay went too far. Apparently, her pet name for him in Klingon wasn't very romantic.

Love dies in strange ways. Sometimes, it's not betrayal it's bad cutlery placement.

Countries with the Weirdest Divorce Laws

Let's take a world tour of "Wait, what?" divorce laws:

- **In the Philippines,** divorce is illegal (except for Muslims). If you want to leave your spouse, you'll need an annulment… and a lot of patience.
- **In Saudi Arabia,** men can divorce their wives simply by saying "I divorce you" three times. Yes, like Beetlejuice, but sadder.
- **In Samoa,** forgetting your wife's birthday is grounds for divorce. Honestly? Fair.
- **In France,** you can (and someone did) divorce a dead person. Yep. A woman married her fiancé *posthumously* and later filed to be… posthumously single.

The world may be round, but love laws? They're wonderfully warped.

Divorce Parties and "Freedom Cakes"

Once upon a time, divorce was whispered over boxed wine and legal pads. Now? It's celebrated with cake, confetti, and karaoke renditions of "I Will Survive."

Welcome to the age of **divorce parties** complete with themes, party favors, and guest lists carefully curated to exclude your ex.

Some wild highlights:

- **"Til Death or Divorce" cake toppers** showing a bride karate-kicking the groom.
- **Piñatas shaped like wedding rings** filled with chocolate and (symbolically) resentment.
- One woman threw a party where everyone wore *black* and danced around her burning wedding dress like it was a bonfire for bad decisions.

Because nothing says healing like a DJ, a taco bar, and a cardboard cutout of your ex that guests can punch.

Love After Love (After Lawyers)

Now that the ink is dry and the freedom cake has been consumed, the big question looms: **Now what?** Do you join a convent? Move to Bali? Rescue shelter dogs until you die?

Or do you... date again?

Fun Fact: How Long Before People Start Dating Again?

Statistically, the average divorced person starts dating again **within 6 months to 2 years.** That range depends on several factors:

- Whether you're the dumper or dumpee
- How many "Eat, Pray, Wine" phases you go through
- Whether your kids are still calling your ex "Daddy" while you scream into a pillow

But here's the fun part: There's *no right time.* One woman I interviewed said she started dating a week later and met "the love of her post-divorce life" at a bar called The Lonely Giraffe. Another waited five years and finally swiped right on her now-husband while sitting in a laundromat.

The truth? Healing doesn't follow a timeline. It follows… tequila. And maybe a therapist.

Real Rebound Stories Awkward, Sweet, and Inspiring

- **Awkward:** One man confessed his first date post-divorce ended when he accidentally called the woman by his ex-wife's name. Her response? "I'll take that as a compliment," she said then ghosted him immediately.

- **Sweet:** A woman met a fellow divorcé at a mutual friend's "I'm single again" bash. Their first date was at IKEA. If you can survive an IKEA trip without a fight, you're basically married already.

- **Inspiring:** A dad of three joined a single-parent hiking group. "I thought I was there to meet other single dads," he said. "Turns out, I met my future wife on top of a mountain. Literally."

Rebounds can be messy. But they can also be the trampoline that launches you higher than you were before.

Dating Apps for Divorcées (Yes, There's One for Co-Parents Too)

Welcome to the jungle: Dating apps! But fear not they're not all twenty-somethings posing with fish and flexing in gym mirrors.

Here are some apps that cater to the newly solo and possibly cynical:

- **Divorce Force** – It's not a dating app, but a support community. Perfect for when you're still crying into nachos.

- **Silver Singles** – A classy option if you're over 50 and over your ex.

- **Stir** – Yes, it's real. This app is for *single parents only*. No child-free folk allowed. Bonus: They have icebreakers like "Who's the better parent Daniel Tiger or Ms. Rachel?"

- **The League** – For those who want a second chance *and* someone with a master's degree.

Because finding love again isn't just about chemistry it's about compatibility, co-parenting calendars, and who brings snacks to soccer practice.

Divorce Glow-Ups

You've heard of revenge bodies. But post-divorce glow-ups? Those are *spiritual*. It's not just about hitting the gym. It's about hitting your stride.

Why Some People Become Their Best Selves Post-Breakup

When you're no longer part of a *"we,"* you rediscover *"me."* And sometimes, that version of you is someone you forgot existed or someone your ex seriously underestimated.

Reasons for the glow-up:

- You finally have time. Like, *uninterrupted* time. No more, "Can you pick up his dry cleaning?"

- You make decisions alone. Want a dog? A tattoo? A shelf of crystals? Go for it.

- You reclaim space. Your closet, your bed, your playlist (RIP to your ex's Nickelback phase).

Post-divorce is when people start yoga, run marathons, write books, take pole-dancing classes, or dye their hair neon green and feel fabulous doing it.

Because *freedom is flattering.*

The Psychology Behind Post-Divorce Confidence

Psychologists call it "identity expansion." After a breakup, people often explore new aspects of themselves, leading to greater self-confidence.

Even science agrees when you're forced to rebuild, you often build back better. It's like an emotional HGTV show: **Extreme Makeover: Self Edition.**

Also, once you've survived a custody hearing *or* divided a DVD collection with a straight face, you feel like you can handle *anything*

Stats on Remarriage: Who's Doing It, Who's Skipping It, and Why

According to the Pew Research Center:

- Two-thirds of divorced people remarry
- Men are more likely to remarry than women
- The average time between divorce and remarriage is about 3.5 years

But more and more people are saying, *"Eh, once was enough."*

Especially women, who often find life post-divorce to be a combo of peaceful, productive, and delightfully pants-optional.

Still, if the right person comes along who won't steal your fries or gaslight you about laundry it's game on.

Kids, Co-Parenting, and Comic Relief

Let's be real: co-parenting can be a logistical nightmare. But it can also be a comedic goldmine.

Because when you're shuttling kids between homes, navigating school projects, and texting your ex about lice outbreaks, sometimes you just have to laugh.

Hilarious Co-Parenting Mishaps

- One mom accidentally texted her ex a grocery list meant for her boyfriend. He replied, "I'm not buying almond milk for your new man."

- A dad showed up to Career Day in a full Batman costume because he thought it was *Superhero Day*. It wasn't. But he became a legend among the kids.

- A mom picked up the wrong twin from daycare and didn't notice until they were halfway home. "In my defense, they were both wearing dinosaur pajamas."

Co-parenting is less about perfection and more about survival. Bonus points for memes and wine.

Celebs Who Nailed the Co-Parenting Game

If movie stars with stylists, nannies, and tequila brands can make it work, so can the rest of us.

Celebrity co-parenting MVPs:

- **Gwyneth Paltrow & Chris Martin** – Invented "conscious uncoupling" and now vacation together with their new spouses. Extra points for Goop-level grace.

- **Jennifer Garner & Ben Affleck** – Despite *everything*, she still lets him borrow her car and picks him up from rehab. That's devotion.

- **Bruce Willis & Demi Moore** – Lived together with their adult kids during quarantine. The group selfies? *Iconic.*

Proof that even in Hollywood, *divorced doesn't mean dysfunctional.*

Fun Fact: Kids of Divorce Are Often More Emotionally Intelligent

Multiple studies show that children of divorce often:

- Develop empathy earlier

- Learn conflict resolution skills
- Become more adaptable

Sure, they may have two Christmases and a complex relationship with packing their backpack, but they also grow up understanding that love can shift. And that's okay.

Turns out, resilience comes with a silver lining.

Bonus Ending: Love Isn't Dead, It's Just Rebranded

So, what have we learned?

We've learned that divorce can be bizarre (hello, haunted spouses), empowering (goodbye, emotional vampires), and even hilarious (freedom cake, anyone?).

We've learned that dating again is weird *and* wonderful.

That glow-ups are real. And those kids? Surprisingly okay.

But most importantly: **Love isn't dead.** It just got a glow-down, a therapy session, and a better haircut.

If you're divorced, divorcing, or daydreaming about running off with a barista named Diego take heart. You're not broken.

You're just… updating your software.

And maybe *just maybe* the next version of love will come with better terms and conditions.

We (Ben and Nicci) hope that we put a smile on your face and a giggle in your throat with this fun book. Thank you for the time. Live, Laugh, and Love ALWAYS.